Your Towns and C

Bristol
IN THE GREAT WAR

This book is dedicated to my mother and father, both of whom know Bristol well.

Your Towns and Cities in the Great War

Bristol
IN THE GREAT WAR

Jacqueline Wadsworth

Pen & Sword
MILITARY

First published in Great Britain in 2014 by
Pen & Sword Military
An imprint of
Pen & Sword Books Ltd
47 Church Street
Barnsley
South Yorkshire
S70 2AS

Copyright © Jacqueline Wadsworth 2014

ISBN 978 1 78303 635 6

The right of Jacqueline Wadsworth to be identified as Author of this work has been asserted by her in accordance with the Copyright, Designs and Patents Act 1988.

A CIP catalogue record for this book is
available from the British Library.

All rights reserved. No part of this book may be reproduced or transmitted in any form or by any means, electronic or mechanical including photocopying, recording or by any information storage and retrieval system, without permission from the Publisher in writing.

Designed by Factionpress

Printed and bound in England
By CPI Group (UK) Ltd, Croydon, CR0 4YY

Pen & Sword Books Ltd incorporates the Imprints of Pen & Sword Aviation, Pen & Sword Family History, Pen & Sword Maritime, Pen & Sword Military, Pen & Sword Discovery, Pen & Sword Politics, Pen & Sword Atlas, Pen & Sword Archaeology, Wharncliffe Local History, Wharncliffe True Crime, Wharncliffe Transport, Pen & Sword Select, Pen & Sword Military Classics, Leo Cooper, The Praetorian Press, Claymore Press, Remember When, Seaforth Publishing and Frontline Publishing.

For a complete list of Pen & Sword titles please contact
PEN & SWORD BOOKS LIMITED
47 Church Street, Barnsley, South Yorkshire, S70 2AS, England
E-mail: enquiries@pen-and-sword.co.uk
Website: www.pen-and-sword.co.uk

Contents

Acknowledgements

I would like to extend my sincere thanks to the many people whose help, interest, time and generosity made writing this book such a pleasure:
Ray Bulmer at Frenchay Village Museum, Dawn Dyer and Jane Bradley of Bristol Reference Library's Local Studies Team, Steve Fell of the Shirehampton Book of Remembrance website, David Hardill at Yate and District Heritage Centre, Pete Insole of Myers-Insole Local Learning, Dr C. S. Knighton at Clifton College, Stella Man at Glenside Hospital Museum, David Read of the Soldiers of Gloucestershire Museum, and Meg Wise at Thornbury Museum.
To Anton Bantock for his excellent articles in the Malago Society magazines, and Lorna Brooks for her Great War research at Yate and District Heritage Centre.
For sharing their Great War stories, images and expertise: Christopher Bigwood, Jackie Carpenter, Pete de Claire, Paula Clutterbuck, Dr Raymond Cooper, Roger Day (who has written his own book *The West Kennet Valley in the Great War*), Helen Frost, Eric Garrett (who has written his own book about the Parish of Olveston during the Great War), Bob Griffin, Brenda Hardingham, Linda Morris, John Penny, Matthew Richardson, Betty Siddell, Andy Summerhayes, Ted Wood, Ken Young.
I am indebted to Jack Williams, who allowed me to use his marvellous material from east Bristol and took time to read my draft manuscript, and to Christine and Mike Lillington who not only shared their own family stories but also pointed me towards other lines of research.
I couldn't have managed without Catherine Dunn for her technical help with the book's images.
Picture credits are given in the captions. Where the name of an organisation is long, abbreviations have been used and the full names can be found at the end of the book under Other Research Sources.
Thank you to Wadard Books, Farningham, Kent (wadardbooks@btinternet.com) for getting my research off to a flying start by selling me the invaluable *Bristol and the Great War* at a price within my range.
And finally, thank you to my husband Ralph, daughters Frances and Catherine, and my parents, Margaret and Bill Wadsworth, for their suggestions, proof reading and invaluable support.

Chapter One

1914 – A Rush of Excitement

Pre-war Bristol was a city full of optimism and enterprise. *[Bob Griffin]*

AS THE SUMMER OF 1914 spread its warmth over the rolling hills of south-west England, the city of Bristol was buzzing with optimism and enterprise. On the shores of the Severn Estuary at Avonmouth Docks a new world was being opened up to ordinary people by two magnificent steamers, the *Royal Edward* and the *Royal George*, which were making regular and affordable trips across the Atlantic. The fortnightly service was advertised as the 'fastest to Canada' and the operator, Royal Line, promised exciting opportunities in a land of prairies and sunshine for those willing to make the move. It was an attractive proposition that

A poster advertising the steamship service to Canada.

thousands of families were taking up, including many Bristolians.

A few miles east of the docks, at the village of Filton on the city's northern fringes, the son of a Bristol painter and decorator was carrying out pioneering work in the field of aeronautics. George White had been inspired by the American Wright brothers' first powered flight in 1903, and with the support of family members he had set up the British and Colonial Aeroplane Company. The first aeroplane to be turned out was the Boxkite, which drew huge crowds to watch spectacular flying displays over the Downs. Soon the company boasted the largest aircraft factory in the world with customers as far afield as Russia and Australia. It also ran its own pilot-training schools, and any young aviators flying over Bristol during the summer of 1914 would have looked down on scenes of unusual industry on the banks of the River Avon.

For downstream of Clifton Suspension Bridge, in the shadow of the bonded warehouses at Ashton Meadows, two thousand workmen were preparing for the Bristol International Exhibition, which was to run all summer and was just the sort of opulent event that Edwardians loved. Its theme was 'England through the ages' and pre-fabricated buildings were being erected to house concerts, displays, lectures and pageants. There were medieval streets, 'Shakespeare's England', a reproduction of Bristol Castle and a grand International Pavilion. Fairground rides were being assembled for children as well as cages for real lions and tigers, and when darkness fell the whole site was bathed in new impressive floodlights.

An early Boxkite takes off. *[Airbus]*

Such enterprise was nothing out of the ordinary for Bristol. Tucked away in the rural West Country, far from the commerce of London and the industry of the north, the city had always pursued its own opportunities and over the centuries had developed a rich and colourful history. In the coming months the aeroplanes of Filton, the passenger ships at Avonmouth and the International Exhibition would all make names for themselves, but as the dark clouds of war drifted in from Europe it would not be as their proprietors had planned.

Countdown to the opening of Bristol International Exhibition.
[BRL, Bristol Times and Mirror]

Floodlights illuminate the International Exhibition site at night.
[Bob Griffin]

Despite the optimism of entrepreneurs, not all Bristolians shared such a rosy vision of the future. Life was a struggle in many working class areas such as those that had grown up around the coalfields of east Bristol and north Somerset. Row upon row of tightly-packed houses had been built the previous century, with little regulation, to house the influx of workers coming in from the depressed countryside. Many of these homes were declining into slums. Typical was Brewer's Place (now demolished) at the end of a small alley in Bedminster, where sixteen houses stood around a small square with four communal toilets at one end. Families of up to ten lived in two rooms and everyone did their washing in the open. A post-war housing report would promise 'to rid the city of these dark alleys' and referred to them as 'dwelling-places with which the sun is not familiar'.

It went without saying that poverty was rife in these areas, especially now that the mines were becoming uneconomic and closing. One of the

Bristol's dark alleys and slums.
[BRL, City and County of Bristol 1919-1930 Housing Report]

few south Bristol pits still open in the summer of 1914 was at South Liberty Lane, Ashton Vale, but even here work was irregular and weeks could go by without men being paid. 'At these times, we ate what we could. We used to catch birds and snails and fry them in the lime kilns opposite Castle Farm,' recalled Vic Hill, the son of a family of twelve from Bishopsworth, which relied on mining.

For many men, the war would provide an opportunity to escape lives that were barely tolerable.

* * *

The speed with which Europe descended into war took many by surprise. Few would have known much about the small Balkan state of Serbia (or Servia as it was then known), where the assassination of Archduke Franz Ferdinand on 28 June 1914 lit the fuse of conflict. Nor would they have understood the complex political alliances that subsequently set European powers on a collision course with each other. But when Britain issued an ultimatum on 4 August demanding that Germany withdraw from Belgium, the seriousness of the situation was clear for all to see.

That evening a crowd gathered outside the offices of the *Bristol Evening Times* and *Echo* to await developments. When the announcement came at 11 pm that war had been declared, the newspaper reported frantic scenes outside:

> 'Newsboys rushed into the streets with placards on which, in flaring type, the simple fact was announced. Papers were eagerly snatched up – as fast as the boys could hand them out they were sold – and the crowd, which had by now assumed large dimensions read the stirring news in silence. Then, almost spontaneously, they commenced cheering and a moment later, bare-headed, they sang the National Anthem. Then, with several placards held high, they marched in orderly fashion through the principal streets of the town, alternately singing God Save the King and patriotic songs.'

The news spread quickly. On the southern outskirts of Bristol it arrived at Bishopsworth on posters pasted on the side of a horse-drawn mail van. For one villager, Edwin Wyatt, it came as a deep disappointment. Just a few days earlier he had written in his diary: 'War between Austria and Serbia began this week; feared lest other nations should become involved, perhaps England, tho' hope not.' Wyatt would use his journal to chart the

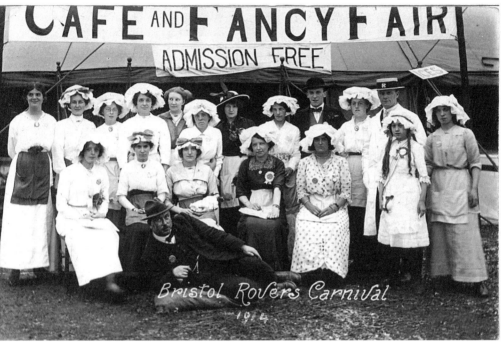

Summer traditions continued despite the looming war.

devastating effect the war had on his village, but for the time being he recorded that life continued as normal with preparations for the harvest festival, choir practice, and croquet matches on the vicarage lawn.

The traditions of summer were being enjoyed elsewhere too, with the usual carnivals, picnics and trips to the seaside. In August 1914 *Frenchay Parish Magazine* reported on a village outing to the coast by rail:

'With reserved compartments and without any change of train we journeyed to Weston in high glee and great comfort ... On arrival we went in a body up to the sea front where at Huntley's Restaurant some luncheon was served out to each child; then we scattered, each to follow our own sweet will and sample the countless seaside attractions till at 4 pm we all met again at the same place to sit down to a capital tea.'

The day ended as blissfully as it had begun:

'The evening was lovely with a glorious sunset. We got back to Stapleton Road about 8.45 pm, and the faithful wagon awaited the happy, if weary, youngsters, with clay-clogged boots and stockings filled with sand, their pockets crammed with seaweed,

Harvesting at Frenchay, but carefree days were soon to end. *[FVM]*

shells, moribund baby crabs and red sticks of peppermint rock, and the inevitable "Present from Weston" tied in what was the morning's clean handkerchief.'

Sadly, Frenchay's carefree summers were drawing to a close and the parish magazine for September would make much grimmer reading:

'The Special Intercession Service for those in peril, need, or sorrow, owing to the War, will be continued on Friday evenings at 8 o'clock till further notice.'

* * *

The people of Britain were at a loss to know quite how their lives would be affected by conflict. Having been at peace with Europe for a century nobody had experienced anything like it and suspicion was everywhere. Civilians kept watch for signs of German sabotage and everyone was on the lookout for spies. Bristol scouts mounted a night-time guard at the Suspension Bridge and looked forward to being served warming cocoa and biscuits for their troubles. Railway staff stood sentry at tunnels and ventilation shafts, often armed only with pick-axe handles. It was a job soldiers later took over, such as those of the Loyal North Lancashire Regiment, who were based at Chipping Sodbury and guarded the rail line to Avonmouth. The loud clanging of cooling rail joints spooked many a soldier who quickly turned his gun on the offending section of rail. Tragically, one young Lancashire private met his end when he was killed by an express train on 19 August, just two weeks after war was declared. Samuel Cooper, 23, was buried at St John the Baptist Church, Old Sodbury.

As tension in Europe grew, Bristolians began to lay in food stocks with the result that shops were quickly stripped of provisions. Some businesses had to close until goods could be replenished and the deputy lord mayor of Bristol, Mr C. J. Lowe, was forced to issue an urgent warning through the newspapers: 'As scarcity can be caused by excessive buying, the

The funeral of Private Samuel Cooper who was killed while guarding a railway. *[Y&DHC]*

Public are strongly urged to buy, and the Retailers to sell, USUAL QUANTITIES ONLY. If this is done, there is plenty of food for all.'

Panic-buying didn't just affect Bristol, the whole country was in its grip and as costs rose the government had to step in with a schedule of maximum prices, shown below. Prices are given per lb, with today's equivalent prices in brackets.

Granulated sugar, 4d (£1.63)
Lump sugar, 5d (£2.04)
Butter, 1s 6d (£7.33)
Colonial cheese, 9?d (£3.86)
American lard, 8d (£3.26)
Margarine, 10d (£4.07)
Continental bacon – by the side, 1s 6d (£7.33)

The food scare subsequently settled down, but for ordinary people the first months of war were a matter of waiting to see what would happen.

One man who saw the future much more clearly than most was Lord Kitchener, the newly appointed secretary of state for war. He disagreed with the generally held view that peace would be restored by Christmas, believing the conflict would continue for three years or more and that huge numbers of troops would be needed – far more than Britain's existing regular army and territorial force could supply. Kitchener set his sights on raising an additional 500,000 men, and his appeals for volunteers through newspaper advertisements and posters became a feature of the war.

The initial rush of volunteers in Bristol was so great that the small recruiting office in Colston Street, which had been quite adequate during peacetime, was overwhelmed. The lord mayor hurriedly called a meeting and it was decided that a committee of citizens should run a much larger recruiting centre at Colston Hall. A rota of between ten and twelve

For KING GEORGE and OLD ENGLAND

6th Reserve Battalion Glo'ster Regiment,
HEADQUARTERS :—ST. MICHAEL'S HILL

JOIN THE SIXTH

More RECRUITS Wanted

Complete Uniform issued immediately on Enlistment.
HEIGHT—5 ft. 5 ins. and upwards.

Apply at Headquarters—Any Day, between 9 a.m. and 5 p.m. ;
Tuesdays, between 6 and 8 p.m.

GOD SAVE THE KING

A call for army volunteers in the Bristol Times and Mirror. *[BRL]*

doctors would be on hand to examine volunteers each day between 8 am and 8 pm, and refreshments were laid on for those who turned up hungry but with no money for food. It was nothing for some young men to walk in from country towns like Thornbury, 12 miles away.

There was great excitement among the would-be recruits as they queued to be checked for height (over 5ft 3in), age (over 18 to enlist and 19 to fight abroad), teeth (strong enough to bite the iron-like ration biscuit) and eyes (able to sight a rifle). Initially standards were fairly rigorous and not all volunteers were accepted, but as the war wore on and fewer men came forward, so requirements would be relaxed.

The reasons for enlisting were many and varied and depended on personal circumstances. For those on the breadline, a job in the army or navy would provide perhaps the first decent, regular wage they had ever been paid. For those whose lives were dominated by long shifts in factories, at the docks, or on the railways, war offered an escape from the daily grind – an adventure abroad. In the words of one jeweller's apprentice, it was an opportunity 'to have six months' holiday at the government's expense'. Little did he know how long his 'holiday' would last. And in areas like east Bristol, where the Easton Colliery had just closed down, war would soak up widespread unemployment.

Patriotism also played an important part in the decision to enlist, and nowhere more so than in Bristol's gentrified suburbs like Redland, Cotham, Sneyd Park and especially Clifton. Here, in the fresh air above the Avon Gorge, wealthy families with servants lived in elegant terraces and villas, and many would have been packing for their annual summer holidays when war was declared. For the men of Clifton duty to their country would have been uppermost in their minds.

Despite the initial excitement, the rush to join up soon began to tail-off despite reports of heavy casualties in Belgium and France. On 24 November Bristol touched what the local press referred to as a 'low-water mark' when only one recruit was enrolled. Maintaining enthusiasm would require stamina on the part of the citizens' recruiting committee – but they were prepared. Advertisements were drawn up using every means possible to encourage men to enlist: 'Men of Bristol think! Do you realise what defeat means? Every man who comes forward now helps to assure our success. Don't wait. If you do, others will, and then you may all be too late,' read one (rather tortuous) plea.

Women were expected to play their part too: 'Ladies, you can influence them; mothers and sisters should be proud to have their sons and brothers serving the country. Use every endeavour to get your relatives and friends to enlist.'

One family in Bedminster could not be faulted for its contribution to the war effort. Charles Turner had eight sons in the army and navy and received a letter of congratulations from Buckingham Palace. The oldest son, Albert, 31, was serving in France with the Royal Field Artillery; the youngest, Herbert, who was just 16, was a signaller in the Royal Naval Barracks at Shotley, Suffolk.

The recruiting campaign marched into the countryside and at Bishopsworth the men of north Somerset heard this speaker's urgent call: 'Our part in this war is not only to vindicate the right of Belgium to her rights and existence, but also to vindicate similar rights of other small nations.' Volunteering afterwards was brisk, perhaps also prompted by reports of atrocities being committed by German soldiers against Belgian civilians.

The *Frenchay Church Magazine*, written largely by Reverend Cyril Travers Burges, did a fine job each month of hectoring able-bodied men who hadn't yet put their names down to serve. One article was highly critical of what it viewed as the complacency of some villagers. It asked how they would react if the Germans invaded Britain, anticipating the colloquial answer: 'They would never come over here, and if they did,' us'ld shute them'.

There was, however, plenty of enthusiasm among men in the parish

Quick march on Frenchay Common: these men are believed to be Frenchay's Volunteer Training Corps.   *[FVM]*

who were unable to fight, either because they were too old or engaged in work of national importance. Like thousands all over the country, they formed a local Volunteer Training Corps for home defence and met in the village hall for drill every Tuesday evening.

Some men in Kingswood were also suspected of shirking their duty, especially those in the boot-making and motor-goods industries that were both important to the war effort. A visitor from the War Office accused them of hiding in factories rather than choosing to volunteer. He went further to say that had they enlisted at the beginning of the war, Britain would not have been forced to retreat from Mons, nor lost so many gallant sons in the first days of the conflict.

Whatever the War Office thought, not all of Kingswood's young men were reluctant to fight, Ewart Mullett welcomed the chance after a childhood that had been fraught with difficulty. He had lost his father at the age of one and although his mother married again, his relationship with his stepfather was not good. As a result Ewart was thrown out on to the streets when he was still a boy and fell in with a bad crowd. At the age of 10 he was detained for 'frequenting the company of reputed thieves' and sent to the National Nautical School For Homeless And Destitute Boys at Portishead. Six years later he made a ten-month voyage to Calcutta as an ordinary seaman aboard the SS *Border Knight*, and was then discharged from the school with a good report.

But the next four years brought disappointment. He was rarely able to obtain work on ships and in 1914 Mullett found himself working as corset-presser in one of the many foundation-wear factories in Kingswood. When war broke out he lost no time in volunteering for the Royal Marines and it was a decision he would never regret. At first Mullett was turned away for being too old (21) and too short (5ft 7in), but as a trained seaman with valuable experience the recruiting officer quietly hinted that he should return later, 'younger and taller', which he did – and was duly recruited.

During the war he served as a gunner with the Royal Marine Artillery aboard the battleship HMS *Canada* and saw action at the Battle of Jutland. A postcard he wrote to his fiancée, Christine Rees, in 1916 after returning to his ship from leave seemed to sum up the contentment he had found: 'I arrived home safe, will write a letter as soon as I can.'

After years as an underdog, Mullett had finally found a life in which he was respected and which gave him some kudos. He survived the war and came back to Bristol where he settled down and married Christine.

Ewart Mullett and his fiancée Christine Rees. Unusual pose, in that the gentleman is seated; perhaps the size of the hat determined this.
[Edna Summerhayes]

Mullett was one of many old boys from the National Nautical School at Portishead who served with the army and navy, and by 1916 the number had already reached 500.

* * *

Military preparations turned Bristol into what felt like a garrison town. As soon as war broke out the regular soldiers of the Gloucestershire Regiment, which had barracks at Horfield on the northern edge of Bristol, were on their way to the fighting. The First Battalion landed in France on 13 August as part of the original British Expeditionary Force and by the end of 1914 they had suffered a large number of casualties. The regiment's Second Battalion, which had been stationed in China, didn't reach the Front until December when exhausted soldiers had already begun digging in for the winter.

Bristol was also the base for several part-time territorial units that had existed solely for home defence before the war. Now they too were being sent to the Front. Among them was the 1st South Midland Brigade, Royal Field Artillery, which lost no time in gathering stores, wagons and 300 horses at the Artillery Ground in Whiteladies Road, ready for despatch. It was all observed with interest – and not a little concern – by Maude Boucher, a mother-of-four who lived nearby in Tyndall's Park Road, Clifton. In a journal that she kept throughout the war, she wrote:

> 'Horses from all parts of the country had been commandeered and some of them had come from the depths of the country and so were not used to much traffic, and the poor things were so frightened of the trams and motor cars, and used to dash across the road from one side to the other – one felt so sorry for the poor animals!

> We went to the bottom of Tyndall's Park Road and saw several of the soldiers off on the Saturday afternoon with numbers of horses and gun carriages. Most of the horses seemed very alarmed and many of the men leading them looked so too. Somebody told us that several horses were taken from farmers at Winscombe [Somerset] at which they grumbled very much, but when all the horses except three or four were returned a few days afterwards as being unfit for the work, they grumbled very much more and were not at all pleased about it.'

Working horses like this one delivering bread in Whitehall were in demand for war service.

The army requisitioned horses from everywhere possible and there were sad tales of Bristolians having to give up animals they depended upon for their livelihoods. Some would fight desperately to keep horses that had become part of the family, but few exceptions were allowed.

Britain's territorial soldiers traditionally looked forward to summer camp each year, and in early August 1914 two units that drew men largely from the Bristol area – the 4th and 6th Battalions, The Gloucestershire Regiment – arrived at Minehead in Somerset for a fortnight under canvas. However, their stay was to be a

Bristol's territorial soldiers were quickly recalled from summer camp at Minehead. *[SoGM, Ref GLRRM:04531.52]*

short one. With war imminent, the battalions were ordered to return to base almost immediately, ending their expedition almost before it had begun. It can't have come as a complete surprise because rumours were circulating even as they departed, but when they arrived back in Bristol it must still have been a shock to see the city so transformed by war.

'Bristolians are on the tip-toe of excitement. And no wonder, for in every direction khaki-clad men are to be seen hurrying hither and thither, and the word WAR is on everybody's lips,' reported the *Bristol Evening News*. 'All the Territorials are mobilising, and are practically ready to answer the call of duty. Crowds of people assembled early this morning outside the various HQs to watch the arrival of the men, and during the day the numbers grow considerably. The sight of soldiers, with fixed bayonets, marching up and down outside the HQs seems to imbue everyone with a patriotic, if not martial, feeling.'

During the days that followed, men of the Territorials bade farewell to their families and departed for training camps in Essex. 'Everywhere handkerchiefs were waved but there was nothing approaching noise, but the glistening eyes of those on either side of Baldwin Street and Victoria Street showed how hearts were beating with hope for the Empire's cause,' wrote a *Bristol Times and Mirror* reporter.

The trains were full of soldiers of all backgrounds, as these two men from the 4/Gloucesters – also known as the 'City of Bristol' Battalion – demonstrate. Sergeant Jack House was a 38-year-old bootmaker from St George who had been married for seventeen years and had a teenage son. He had served in the Boer War of 1899-1902 in South Africa and was a longstanding territorial soldier. By contrast, 20-year-old Edwin Wood was a fresh-faced clerk from Easton who was almost young enough to be House's son. Wood lived at home with his father (another bootmaker), mother, teenage brother and two younger sisters and this was his first experience of army life.

Troop departures were not without incident. One tragic accident occurred when two horses pulling a wagon-full of army baggage took fright and bolted down Park Street in the city centre. They pulled off an overhanging shop blind, smashed the window of another shop, then swerved across the road and collided with a wagonette in which an elderly lady was sitting. The wagonette was overturned and the woman had to be pulled from the wreckage. She later died. One of the horses was led away uninjured, but the other had fallen and broken its leg and had to be put down.

While troops marched to railway stations to board trains an altogether heavier stream of traffic was rumbling through the city towards the port of Avonmouth. Here equipment and vehicles were being loaded on to ships for despatch to the Front. Convoys included ambulances, London omnibuses for troop-transport, and heavy artillery hidden beneath tarpaulins that made them look, rather eerily, like huge harps. These long lines of vehicles caused windows to vibrate as they snaked up Whiteladies Road, over The Downs and down through what were then the country lanes of

Private Edwin Wood was completely new to army life... *[Wood Family]*

... Opposite: Sergeant Jack House, (left), was a veteran of the Boer War . *[SoGM, Ref GLRRM:04531.2]*

Transport wagons pass through Bristol on their way to Avonmouth.
[BRL, Bristol and the War magazine]

Stoke Bishop and Shirehampton. The route was not ideal and many drivers lost their way until Bristol's Recruiting Committee came to the rescue and erected 'To Avonmouth' signposts.

One afternoon Maude Boucher and a friend followed the queues by motor car to see what was happening. As they neared the docks her attention was caught by an army kitchen set up on a roadside. A huge meal was being cooked 'in a most brisk and vigorous manner' for the men who were arriving.

> 'There were about twenty army pots on wooden fires, and the men were chopping great carcases of meat into joints, and some of the meat they were cutting up with large and terrible-looking knives, and putting on to stew. One soldier was peeling onions, and another putting pepper and tomatoes into the pots. They all seemed very cheerful and jolly over it all and appeared to rather enjoy our interest in their culinary preparations.'

Bristol was a city with strong maritime traditions and many would serve at sea as merchant and naval seamen. In the early months of war, men of the city's Royal Naval Volunteer Reserve were sent to Belgium to save Antwerp from falling into German hands. They fought as infantrymen in the new Royal Naval Division, but the mission ended in failure. It was a worrying time for Richard Quick, the superintendent of Bristol Art Gallery, whose son was involved – and a huge relief when he finally received a postcard from him: 'We had to leave Antwerp all in ruins, and were absolutely the last men to leave,' wrote Petty Officer RH Quick. 'As we were driven back and had no artillery to check them with, we had to go into Holland, where we were disarmed. We shall have to stay here till the end of the war.' Quick and his comrades had managed to escape to the Netherlands, but as it was a neutral country they were interned until the conflict was over.

* * *

As 1914 drew to a close, the reality of war was becoming clear. Wounded soldiers were now arriving back at Temple Meads Station, filthy, bloodied and bandaged. One Bristol paper published this soldier's letter, which described conditions at the Front:

> 'In the daytime it is a butcher shop and at night it is like Madam Tussaud's, nothing but dead and wounded, dead horses, burning towns and villages, murderers and refugees ... It is painful to see women and children seeking a place of safety when shells go over and blow them to pieces. We are in a farm at the present time ... and a Belgian refugee is here with three children on his own. His wife got shelled as they were flying for their lives.'

Belgian refugees were now seeking refuge in Britain and Bristol would accommodate 2,000. They were found homes and jobs, education was provided for the children, and money was raised to support them. The first Belgians arrived in the city on 22 September and were cheered by waving crowds. But as they paraded through the centre by tram many looked drained and bewildered.

For some, like Maude Boucher, the culture difference took a bit of getting used to. 'Many of the first arrivals were of the peasant class and most of the women wore large shawls and no hats, and were generally standing at the gates and doors of their homes,' she wrote in her journal. 'The family which came later on to Tyndall's Park were of the better class but had been obliged to leave their homes and had buried most of their possessions and treasures somewhere in Belgium. (That is as the story goes.) They had been able to bring practically nothing with them and as their family consisted of from ten to fifteen children in number, they were very glad of such a comfortable home as was provided for them.'

The Belgians were not the only visitors to Bristol that winter. Five thousand Scottish troops were also billeted in the city when their tented camps in Wiltshire became too wet and muddy to live in. The first to arrive were the Black Watch, many of them volunteers who were still without uniform, and as they marched through the streets with a swinging stride to the skirl of bagpipes, they were given a rousing reception. One newspaper commented on the men's excellent physiques, but added 'they bore the unmistakable evidence of having roughed it during their month or two's sojourn on Salisbury Plain'.

Initially there was alarm at the troops' arrival, with some believing they had been sent because Bristol was about to be invaded. Once those fears had been calmed, a new fear took over that was rather more delicate: the effect the troops were having on local girls. One concerned group, which was led by the president of the Mother's Union, suggested all young women should be back at home before 9 pm each night. Feelings ran so high that she was moved to make a special address at the cathedral, which was reported in the local press:

'I am horrified to notice in our streets large numbers of young girls whose laughter is loud if it is not bold, who seem to be always associating with soldiers, forgetting their dignity

Published Fortnightly.   PRICE ONE PENNY.

BRISTOL AND THE WAR

OCTOBER 3, 1914.

Vol. 1. No. 1.

BELGIAN REFUGEES IN BRISTOL.

Passing through the City en route for Victoria Square, Clifton, where a substantial meal was awaiting them. (Photo, H. C. Stevens, Atley Hill)

Belgian refugees receive a warm welcome in the city centre. [BRL]

Belgian refugees at Yate, many fled their country with nothing. *[Y&DHC]*

Crowds greet soldiers of the Black Watch outside the Colston Hall.
[BRL, Bristol and the War magazine]

and doing and saying things which in ordinary times they would never dream of doing or saying I appeal to you not only for your own sakes but for the sakes of our brave lads who are training, to be strong and clean and pure and self-sacrificing do not let one of us be a stumbling block in the way of strengthening their character and keeping their vision bright. If you do so you are just as much an enemy of your country as any foreign foe.'

Despite the strains caused by a city teeming with strangers, Bristol rose to the occasion and made its visitors feel at home that Christmas. Parties, concerts, and dinners were organised, the licensing justices allowed picture houses to open on Christmas Day (as long as suitable films were shown), a 'Christmas tree party' was attended by 600 Belgians, and ordinary people invited soldiers into their homes to join their families for Christmas lunch. Few could have imagined that they would still be entertaining troops for three more Christmases to come.

Young Bristol girls were urged to be 'strong and clean and pure'.
[Wood Family]

Chapter Two

1915 – War Takes a Grip

THE NEW YEAR OF 1915 began as the old one had ended, wet and miserable. Some demoralised Bristolians suggested that the excessive rainfall had been caused by gunfire on the continent, but the British meteorological authorities did not agree, saying the winter rain of 1914 had been nothing out of the ordinary. In any case, there were now more urgent things to worry about.

In Europe, stalemate had set in along the Western Front and a war of attrition had begun that would last for the next four years. Another Front was opening up in the Mediterranean as the Allies took on the Turks on the rocky Gallipoli peninsula. The aim was to force their way through the Dardanelle Straits and relieve Russian troops, who were under threat from Turkey in the Caucasus. Bristol would play an important part in supplying this campaign, which would end in humiliating defeat for Britain and her allies at the end of the year.

Meanwhile everyday life continued as industriously as ever in Bristol and with no sign of a quick end to the conflict the city had transformed itself, smoothly and swiftly, to meet the needs of war. Nowhere was this more in evidence than at the port of Avonmouth where once-colourful scenes of commerce were replaced by khaki troop movements. The priority now was to dispatch men, equipment and

WEATHER FORECAST

The Bristol and District Forecast for to-day is as follows :—Variable sky, some rain or passing showers; moderate temperature.

The *Bristol Times and Mirror* forecast a wet and miserable start to 1915 *[BRL]*

vehicles to the Front and the following figures illustrate just how much passed through the port during the course of the war:

Ships: 2,279
Personnel: 203,337
Horses and mules: 339,601
Vehicles: 51,166
Tonnage of goods: 1,759,055

Equipment for shipment arrived by rail and road and for those who lived near the docks life changed completely. The narrow streets and lanes that led past their homes became choked with columns of traffic creeping towards the waterside. Before the war Avonmouth's hotels and pubs had served the visiting merchant seamen, but the authorities had made few arrangements for the hundreds of tired and hungry drivers who now waited patiently in their military vehicles. It fell to the vicar of Shirehampton, the Reverend Harold Gibson, and local landowner Napier Miles to ease the situation. They converted a wooden hut beside St Andrew's Church in Avonmouth into a canteen and rest room. It became known as St Andrew's Soldiers' Home and, as the war progressed, similar facilities sprung up in the area, supported by local people.

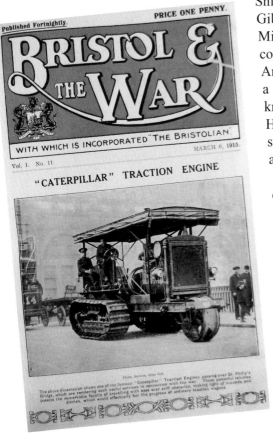

Vast areas of the docks were taken over by new military depots: a mechanical transport depot, a supply depot for stores, and a tractor depot for caterpillar-tracked vehicles, which were proving invaluable on the rough and muddy terrain of France. Developed in America for the agricultural industry, these noisy contraptions were shipped directly from the United States to Avonmouth, overhauled, then sent

A noisy caterpillar tractor is pictured rumbling through the city centre. *[BRL]*

to the Front. Damaged vehicles were returned for repair. The strain on dockyard cranes, which had to lift them, was immense.

The tractor depot was set up on a 50-acre site, which had until then been used by the Petrol Users and Traders Supply Society. Despite the difficulties this caused, the society's manager expressed a patriotic willingness to co-operate: 'Whilst, of course, this would mean a tremendous inconvenience to the Society, still, at the same time, we feel that we should put no difficulties or obstacles in the way,' he wrote in a

Dockyard managers kept a close eye on what the military were up to at Avonmouth. *[Bristol Port Company]*

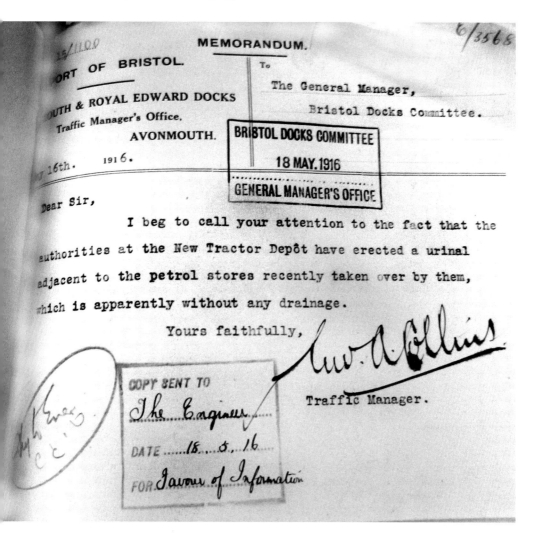

letter to the docks committee.

Documents that record the development of the depot reveal how close an eye the civilian dockyard managers kept on their military counterparts. 'I beg to call your attention to the fact that the authorities at the New Tractor Depot have erected a urinal adjacent to the petrol stores recently taken over by them, which is apparently without any drainage,' the yard's traffic manager informed the docks committee.

Over at the engineer's office there was concern about the military's apparent slackness in maintaining a railway level crossing: 'We have found that they are somewhat casual in keeping the groove clean. Could it be arranged for a watchman at the gate in the fence to look after this to see it is in satisfactory condition.' A reply was promptly dispatched from the yard superintendent's office: 'The watchman at the gate has instructions to do as the Engineer suggested.'

* * *

The Gallipoli campaign took precedence at Avonmouth during the spring of 1915 and among those dispatched to the Mediterranean was the war poet Rupert Brooke, who served with the Royal Naval Division. He set sail for the Dardanelles aboard the *Grantully Castle* but survived only two months. After contracting dysentery in Egypt he died on 23 April and was buried on the Greek island of Skyros.

So busy was Avonmouth that in one eight-day period during April 1915, a total of 10,000 men, 9,000 horses and mules, and 536 vehicles were dispatched aboard seventeen transport ships. Among the troops were twenty-five young farmers from the Severn Vale, north of Bristol, who belonged to the Old Down Troop of the Royal Gloucestershire Hussars. The Hussars were part of the Yeomanry – the mounted arm of the territorial force – and the Old Down Troop was formed in 1906 by two local army officers, Charles Turner of Old Down House at Tockington, and Algar Howard of Thornbury Castle. Standards were high and only those with the best horses – agile, fit and fast – were accepted. It went without saying that the recruits were experienced horsemen who used animals for work and transport on their farms.

Membership of the troop offered young farmers a chance to socialise away from the land they were tied to. On high days and holidays they paraded on horseback through the parish in full dress uniform, quickening the pulses of local young ladies. And every May they enjoyed a two-week

Old Down troopers at Thornbury Station returning from a pre-war summer camp. *[Eric Garrett]*

summer camp, travelling to different parts of the country with their horses, often by train from Thornbury Station.

When the Old Down farmers arrived at Avonmouth they had already been away from the Severn Vale for nearly a year, training on the sandy beaches of Norfolk to prepare for deployment in the Middle East. The women had taken over the running of the farms and children helped with the poultry and pigs. Some families had said goodbye to more than one man: brothers Arthur and Frank Garrett, of Washingpool Farm, Easter Compton, were both in the Old Down Troop, as was their cousin Colin, who farmed land on the edge of Thornbury.

While training in Norfolk, Frank Garrett had experienced some early excitement when locals discovered a bomb that had been dropped by a German Zeppelin. He was sent to investigate and returned with the device in a wheelbarrow. It was placed on the lawn of the country house where his troop was billeted and the men took turns to stand guard until explosive experts arrived to take it away. By this time a large crowd had gathered, including the village bobby, all wanting a closer look and to have their photograph taken with it.

The Old Down farmers set sail from Avonmouth on 10 April, squashed on to crowded decks. They fought at Gallipoli, then Palestine, and returned at the end of the war with thrilling tales of dawn cavalry charges made with swords drawn. Happily, all but one of their original number survived, including the Garretts, although Arthur had contracted malaria and Frank was wounded in the shoulder.

In the years before the war shipbuilding had been flagging at Avonmouth, but the conflict gave it an unexpected – if not to say welcome

Grainy snapshots show the Royal Gloucestershire Hussars on cramped decks as they sail from Avonmouth for Gallipoli. *[Eric Garrett]*

– boost. Three additional berths were opened by Charles Hill and Sons at their Albion Dockyard to maintain Britain's war fleet and workers were kept busy refitting merchant ships for war and repairing damaged vessels.

Among those refitted were a fleet of much-loved paddle steamers, which for years had taken families on summer excursions up and down the Bristol Channel. The steamers belonged to P and A Campbell's White Funnel Fleet and all thirteen were requisitioned for war. Once repainted in drab camouflage they were hardly recognisable. Their various missions included sweeping for mines, chasing submarines, assisting in salvage, and they were often shelled and bombed by aircraft. The steamers worked in the Atlantic, the North Sea, on the Irish coast and in the English Channel, as well as the Thames Estuary and Moray Firth. One, the *Barry*, served as far afield as the Dardanelles and it was probably this vessel that turned up unexpectedly at Alexandria, Egypt, in August 1915, much to the delight of Bristolians of the Royal Gloucestershire Hussars who were waiting to depart for Gallipoli. 'The boat we went in was oddly enough a Bristol pleasure-steamer: much appreciated by the Bristol Troop!' wrote Second Lieutenant Edgerton Cripps in his diary.

Sadly, two paddle-steamers were lost, both with names that sounded as if they should have provided protection in themselves: the *Brighton Queen* and the *Lady Ismay*. However, at the end of the war the *Glen Usk* witnessed the surrender of the German fleet, before returning to Bristol and resuming the summer pleasure service with the surviving Campbell steamers.

And what of the two luxury ships that had brought prestige to Bristol during the pre-war years with their speedy service to Canada? The *Royal Edward* and the *Royal George* were converted into troop-carriers, their sumptuous drawing rooms, café-lounges, dining saloons and libraries turned over to servicemen who may or may not have bothered to admire the art nouveau décor. Fate would take the ships in very different directions. While the *Royal George* survived the war the *Royal Edward* had the dubious honour of being the first British troop ship to be sunk.

Her final voyage began when she departed from Avonmouth in July 1915 for the Dardanelles with 1,367 officers and men, plus 220 mainly-local crew. As she headed for the Greek island of Lemnos after two weeks at sea, she was torpedoed by a German submarine. Within three minutes her decks were awash, and within six minutes she sank, bows up. Hundreds of lives were lost. One survivor who jumped into the sea recalled fighting the terrifying suction that was drawing him under. When he surfaced the sea was full of 'wreckage and men yelling like mad'. It was reported that many had been below decks re-stowing their kit after a lifeboat drill when the torpedo struck, which may have contributed to the great loss of life. A nearby hospital ship helped rescue survivors.

Today at the Port of Bristol Seafarers' Centre at Portbury, a brass plaque commissioned by the Royal Edward Athletic and Social Club

The *Bristol Times and Mirror* breaks the news of the *Royal Edward* sinking. *[BRL]*

The *Royal Edward*, formerly a luxury steamer, was the first British troop ship to be sunk. *[BRL, Bristol and the War magazine]*

ROYAL EDWARD TORPEDOED

DISASTER IN AEGEAN SEA.

1,600 ON BOARD

ONLY 600 REPORTED SAVED.

The Secretary of the Admiralty makes the following announcement:—
The British transport Royal Edward was sunk by an enemy submarine in the Ægean Sea last Saturday morning.

According to the information at present available, the transport had on board 32 military officers and 1,350 troops, in addition to the ship's crew of 220 officers and men.

The troops consisted mainly of reinforcements for the 29th Division and details of the Royal Army Medical Corps.

Full information has not yet been received, but it is known that about 600 have been saved.

commemorates thirty-five members of the ship's catering department who drowned. Many were Bristol boys who worked as stewards, cooks, storekeepers, scullions, butchers, a pantryman and a baker.

* * *

Not surprisingly, the entrance to the Bristol Channel – a major shipping route into and out of England – bristled with German submarine activity during the war and was kept under constant surveillance by small naval vessels. Signal stations also kept watch and the one at Walton Bay, Clevedon, was manned by Bristol sea scouts who did a sterling job throughout the war, even though occasionally enthusiasm got the better of them. From time to time they would contact the nearby Portishead gun battery to report a suspicious object floating up the channel only for the guns to open fire on a tree trunk or a lump of old wreckage. Still, better safe than sorry.

Security at the port was understandably tight and photography was strictly prohibited, although information still managed to get out. One soldier who was based there wrote to his 12-year-old brother: 'You would like to be here for a day or two just to have a look round the docks and see the ships being loaded and unloaded. The other day they were loading bombs, they look just like footballs in the distance but packed separately in pieces of board.'

The enemy would certainly have relished a closer look at an odd-looking contraption that was being shipped to France from Avonmouth – the tank. Although unreliable in its early days, it represented the cutting-edge of technology and Bristol men were queuing up to have a go according to one report: 'Numerous local soldiers volunteered for the hazardous and weird task of manning His Majesty's Land Ships.'

* * *

Amid the noise and fumes of military vehicles, the more natural sound of clattering hooves could also be heard in the congested lanes around Avonmouth. It came from horses and mules being driven up to meadows around Shirehampton where a remount depot had been established. Although motor transport was now in regular use at the Front, horses were still needed by the cavalry and to haul heavy goods and artillery but the numbers requisitioned at home were insufficient to meet demand. Animals were therefore being shipped in from the Americas. The Shirehampton depot could hold up to 5,000 horses and was one of four principal remount centres in Britain (the others were in Hampshire and Lancashire).

Once put ashore the animals would be run through the streets in droves, and one contemporary account described convoys of mules being led by men clad in sheepskin-fronted trousers. The roads were left thick with manure and after a shower of rain became slippery and dangerous. Water carts were used to spray disinfectant.

The remount depot consisted of large fields for grazing plus long lines of huts that accommodated men, blacksmiths, shops, cookhouses, offices, fodder, and of course stabling for horses. There was a large veterinary hospital on site, plus a disinfectant bath to treat mange.

Here the animals would be rested, quarantined and checked for fitness before being sent for work at home or abroad. A total of 347,045 horses and mules would pass through the depot during the war and by all accounts they were well looked after, although nothing could alleviate the suffering on the long sea voyages. According to Private Charles Day, who worked at the camp in 1916, around 900 to 1,100 were carried in each ship. 'It is good class of horses that come, nice clean legged ones just right to do some work by the look of them, but look tough and dirty when

Huts at the Shirehampton Remount Depot in 1919, sketched by Bristol illustrator Samuel Loxton. *[BRL, Ref: D302]*

they come off the boats for perhaps they have been on the water several weeks,' he wrote.

Conditions inside the ships were grim: 'All packed in very tightly together, only just room for them all to stand. There are three or four lots, one above the other, and when you get down into the bottom of the ship it is so hot and smells horrible, almost takes your breath away.' As Private Day wrote his letter, the arrival of seven ships full of horses and mules was imminent. It should have been eight but sadly one had gone down.

The depot was initially staffed by civilians who worked under army officers but by 1915 it had become a military unit. Many of the soldiers were experienced horsemen like Charles Day who had worked as a dairyman in Wiltshire, although in a letter to his mother he said that he had told an officer he knew nothing about horses as he felt it was better the army teach him everything he needed to know.

Another experienced horseman was Corporal Harry Poole who arrived at Shirehampton in 1918 and remained there until 1919. Earlier in the war he had served with the Royal Horse Guards cavalry regiment but for some reason was invalided out. He then served with the Army Veterinary Corps and was attached to the veterinary hospital at Shirehampton. It is likely that this is where the photograph overleaf was taken showing Poole in uniform and his men in mucky overalls with the stabling behind them.

Poole maintained his link with the equestrian world after the war when he worked in Staffordshire as a gamekeeper for Sir Geoffrey Congreve, an accomplished racehorse owner and trainer whose horse Lazy Boots came fourth in the 1935 Grand National.

Parts of the Shirehampton Remount Depot were on low-lying ground that became swampy during wet winters and some horses died in the unhealthy conditions. Conditions were similar at a smaller depot near the Ashton Halt rail stop south of Bristol, where animals from all over the Mendips were collected in a farmer's yard to be sent on to Avonmouth. A cider press had been removed to make room for them and at night the villagers of Bishopsworth could hear whinnying as horses and mules trampled the muddy ground into a quagmire. Here too many died.

Concern about conditions at Shirehampton prompted questions to be asked in the House of Commons but the under-secretary of state for war was quick to refute criticism. 'Considering the large number of horses that have been landed at Avonmouth after a winter Atlantic voyage, the

Harry Poole on horseback (before he received his corporal's stripes).
[Helen Frost]

Corporal Harry Poole in uniform with his men, probably at Shirehampton. *[Helen Frost]*

percentage of deaths (0.65) is extraordinarily small,' he replied.

Although some accounts of war horses' lives make upsetting reading, the British rarely allowed their animals to suffer unnecessarily. One national newspaper published a report from an equine hospital in northern France that was run by the Army Veterinary Corps and could accommodate nearly 2,000 injured animals. Batches of sixty to a hundred would arrived by train, suffering mainly from shrapnel and bullet wounds, and after treatment they were allowed to rest and graze at convalescent camps before being returned to the Front.

The Shirehampton Remount Depot was dismantled in 1919 and Bristol Corporation bought some of the huts to relieve the city's housing shortage. The only reminder today is Barracks Lane, off Avonmouth Road, which once would have echoed to the clatter of horses' hooves.

* * *

The first wounded soldiers to arrive at Temple Meads Station, on 2 September 1914, were 120 men from the Battle of Mons and there to greet them, serve refreshments and drive them to hospital were volunteers who would welcome new arrivals throughout the war under the auspices of the Red Cross. Between 1914 and 1918 a total of 412 trains would bring 69,411 wounded servicemen to Bristol. Ambulance trains often arrived in the early morning hours but volunteers still turned out, even if they had day jobs to go to.

Under emergency plans drawn up during peacetime, Bristol was scheduled to provide 520 beds for the war-wounded (in military parlance these formed the 2nd Southern General Hospital), and the beds would be at the Royal Infirmary and Southmead Infirmary. Within weeks of war being declared, however, it became clear that this would be nowhere near enough to meet demand, especially with a civilian population that still expected hospital beds when they needed them. From then on facilities in and around Bristol were constantly expanding.

Extensions were added to Southmead Infirmary, one of which was under canvas, and new auxiliary hospitals were opened where soldiers were sent to convalesce. Run by the Red Cross, many of these were established in country houses and the owners often became involved in running them. The first to open its doors in Bristol was at Cleve House, Downend, the home of Sir Charles Cave and his wife. It was staffed by nurses of the local Voluntary Aid Detachment, assisted by the Queen Alexandra's Imperial Military Nursing Service (the nursing branch of the British Army). The kitchen was run by civilians.

Judging from photographs kept by two of the nurses, sisters Molly and Nancy Elliot, the soldiers had a lot of fun while recovering there. They are shown in hospital blues (as hospital uniform was known) relaxing in the Cleve House garden, spectating at Downend Cricket Club, enjoying a fancy dress whist drive, and setting off on a day trip to Badminton in cars driven by the local gentry. Today Cleve House is no longer standing.

Other fine Bristol homes that were turned into hospitals included Ashton Court, which accommodated wounded officers, and King's Weston House at Lawrence Weston. At Stoke Bishop, a wealthy and generous couple called Robert and Marjorie Bush converted their home, Bishop's Knoll, into a hospital for Australian soldiers and ran it at their

Wounded soldiers at Cleve Hill Hospital enjoy a laugh in the garden (above) while others share a light-hearted moment with laundry staff. *[FVM]*

own expense – Mr Bush had been a sheep farmer in Australia for thirty-five years. The Red Maids' School at Westbury-on-Trym was turned into a 200-bed hospital, and at Greenbank a magnificent new sports pavilion belonging to Packer's chocolate factory was converted to take in recovering soldiers.

But although Bristol's extensive hospital network spread well beyond the city boundaries, there was still an urgent need for more beds. A solution was found when Bristol Lunatic Asylum at Fishponds was converted into a new war hospital. Built in the mid-1800s, this imposing institution had expanded enormously during the Victorian era and housed cases ranging from people with psychiatric problems to homosexuals, alcoholics and epileptics. Now, with little notice, these inmates were transferred to other hospitals in the south-west and the asylum was converted into the Beaufort War Hospital, which opened in May 1915 with 1,460 beds.

Orderlies of the Royal Army Medical Corps helped staff the hospital and among them was a brilliant young artist called Stanley Spencer who was just starting to make a name for himself. A tiny man of 5ft 1in, he arrived at Beaufort in 1915 and was somewhat intimidated by what he

The imposing Beaufort War Hospital, formerly a lunatic asylum. *[GHM]*

first saw. 'The gate was high and massive as the gate of hell. It was a vile cast iron structure,' he later recalled. In letters to friends he described how he lived in fear of a large sergeant major, who punished those who were late for duty or incorrectly dressed. Some of the former asylum inmates had been retained for domestic duties and Stanley praised them as hard workers, adding 'one persists in saluting us and always with the wrong hand'.

Spencer's role as orderly involved everything from cooking and carrying to cleaning and making beds. He observed the details of hospital life closely and after the war used them to paint a series of scenes that give a fascinating glimpse of what life was like. Known as the Beaufort Panels, they can be seen at the Sandham Memorial Chapel in Burghclere, Hampshire. Included are paintings such as Bed-making, in which two patients are wrapped in counterpanes while staff make their beds, Frostbite, which recalls one of Spencer's tasks – scraping the patients' feet, Tea in the Hospital Ward, in which one soldier sits lost in thought amidst the bustle going on around him, and Scrubbing the Floor, in which a man is spread lengthways scrubbing a corridor while orderlies step over him.

A photograph has recently emerged that is thought to show Spencer eating a meal with other medical orderlies at Beaufort. It is one of the few photographs of him during his time at the hospital.

Spencer spent ten months at Fishponds,

Wounded soldiers arrive at Beaufort War Hospital. *[GHM]*

Still in muddy uniforms, new arrivals put on a brave face at Beaufort War Hospital. *[GHM]*

Artist Stanley Spencer is thought to be sitting in the far left row with a lock of hair over his forehead.

leaving in 1916 to serve in Salonika. He was invalided home with malaria in 1918. The Beaufort War Hospital reverted to civilian use after the war and became known as the Glenside Hospital. It closed in 1994 and the building is now used by the University of the West of England.

Much pioneering medical work was carried out in Bristol during the war. The Beaufort Hospital became known for its orthopaedic expertise and surgeons from all over the world came to study its methods. Bristol was also noted for its treatment of typhoid, dysentery, and penetrating wounds of the chest and as an ophthalmic centre for men whose sight was seriously injured. Large numbers passed through to have artificial eyes fitted, although those who were totally blind went to St Dunstan's (now known as Blind Veterans UK).

Although the city's record for treating the wounded was excellent, not all survived and those who died in Bristol hospitals were buried at Arnos Vale Cemetery where they are remembered on a memorial. For those who made a good recovery it didn't take long to rediscover the old pleasures in life, as Maude Boucher of Clifton described in her wartime journal:

'When the weather was fine, the soldiers often used to sit in the greens belonging to the [Southmead] Infirmary and which adjoined it, and the people passing by used to stop and talk to them, and some of them passed them in cigarettes, sweets and other things through the railings. But one day, people – without being seen by anyone in charge – passed whisky and other drinks in to the soldiers and the soldiers in consequence nearly all got intoxicated and the nurses could do nothing with them but had to send for the doctors. After this episode the spaces between the railings were filled up, and some male attendants were added to the Infirmary staff.'

* * *

In happier times trains that were now transporting soldiers to and from the Front would have been filled with passengers on pleasure trips, such as those on their way to visit the Bristol International Exhibition in the summer of 1914. Visitors from all over the country had been expected at Ashton Meadows, but when excursion trains were cancelled to accommodate military traffic the exhibition was forced to close two months early in August.

All was not lost, however. The War Office swiftly bought the site and

'Shakespeare's house' offered stylish accommodation for officers at the White City barracks. *[Bob Griffin]*

Soldiers relax in the White City's reading and recreation room. *[Bob Griffin]*

converted it into a much-needed military base, which quickly became known as the White City because of the copious amounts of whitewash used. With its buildings reflecting the theme 'England through the ages' it provided one of the most stylish army bases in the country. Officers were accommodated in the houses of 'Shakespeare's England', Bristol Castle was turned into barracks for the men, the dance hall was used as a dining room, and the International Pavilion became a huge gymnasium. Local organisations also helped to make the site comfortable, with the Church of England Men's Society furnishing a smart reading and recreation room.

The first soldiers to make the White City their home were those of the 12th Battalion, The Gloucestershire Regiment, also known as Bristol's Own. This was one of the new volunteer battalions that were formed as a result of Kitchener's call for recruits. Independent of the regular army and the territorial force, they were formally known as service battalions although most people simply called them Kitchener's Army.

The Twelfth was different to other service battalions of the Gloucestershire Regiment because it was raised in answer to a call from local men who wanted to serve together. The formation of such units – pals battalions as many became known – was encouraged by the War Office in the hope that more volunteers would come forward if they could serve with friends, workmates or neighbours.

Bristol's Own was not open to any Tom, Dick or Harry. Those invited to join were specified thus: 'The mercantile and professional young men of the city of Bristol and neighbourhood.' Applicants had to be aged 19-

Bristol's Own parade in civvies at Ashton Park, with the International Exhibition still standing in the background. *[Bob Griffin]*

35 and unmarried, and enrolment forms were deposited at the Colston Hall, the Stock Exchange, the Commercial Rooms, banks and insurance companies, and the Constitutional, Liberal and Clifton Clubs. They were not left at factories, mines and railway depots. The reason given was that Bristol was proud of its history in commerce and trade, and it was this class of young men who should be given the opportunity to fight. In reality, a War Office directive had made it clear that white-collar workers could more easily be spared to fight than those in agriculture, mining, engineering or transport.

Recruiting opened on 15 August 1914 and there was a rush to join up at the Colston Hall where cheering crowds watched on. Many men took little notice of the entry restrictions, which prompted the Citizens' Recruiting Committee to state tersely in a letter to the local press: 'It will save the committee a lot of time if those not qualified will refrain from

0th Platoon   Nº3 80. Bristols Own.   Pioneers

Bristol's Own practise trench-digging, Bill Short is fourth left.

[Bob Griffin]

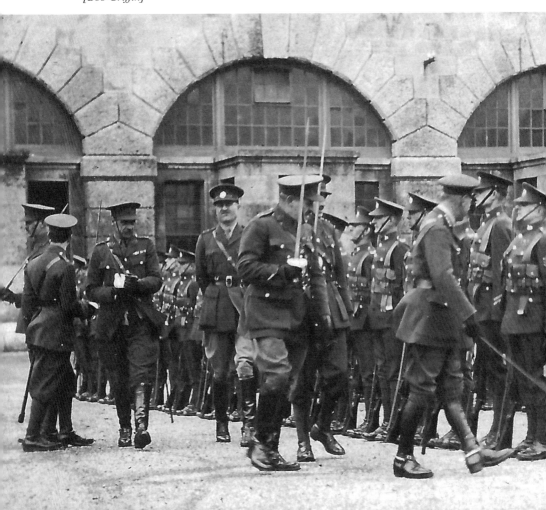

filling up the forms.' However, Bristol's Own was never quite the unit of professionals that was originally intended.

It took just four weeks for a battalion of 1,100 to be raised and for the first few weeks the new recruits lived at home while they waited for conversion work at the White City to be finished. A shortage of uniforms and weapons meant that most simply wore their best suits when they reported for parade each day.

When the battalion finally took up residence at the White City some complained that it was as draughty on the inside as it was stylish on the outside, but the men soon settled down and took stock of those with whom they would serve. Not all were Bristolians. One contingent of eighty came from Weston-super-Mare. There were plenty of tradesmen – shoemakers, cooks and grooms – who were recruited for their specific skills, and

A final inspection for Bristol's Own near Temple Meads Station before taking leave of the city. *[Bob Griffin]*

manual workers who would carry out the battalion's labouring work. Among them was Bill Short of Bedminster who had been employed as a ganger for the Great Western Railway – God's Wonderful Railway as he called it – and would remember plenty of working class men like himself in the ranks of Bristol's Own.

Short managed to side-step another rule of enrolment just before the battalion's departure from Bristol in June 1915. He wed his sweetheart Lillian Thompson and set off for war as a married man.

It must have been an emotional night at the Colston Hall on 25 May 1915 when the city said farewell to Bristol's Own. After months of route marches, rifle and bayonet practice, night operations, sham fights and trench-digging they were finally on their way, first to training camp then to the Front. A song called Bravo Bristol! had been sent to the recruiting committee to help raise funds for the battalion. It was written by the celebrated musicians Fred Weatherly, who came from Portishead, and Ivor Novello, who had found fame by writing, respectively, Danny Boy and Keep the Home Fires Burning. On that final night Bravo Bristol! was sung by everyone:

> It's a rough long road we're going,
> It's a tough long job to do.
> But as sure as the wind is blowing,
> We mean to see it through!
> Who cares how the guns may thunder?
> Who recks of the sword and flame?
> We fight for the sake of England,
> And the honour of Bristol's name!

As the months rolled on other battalions made the White City their base too, like the 14th Battalion, The Gloucestershire Regiment, otherwise known as Bristol's Bantams. Earlier in the war these were men who would have been rejected by the army because they were below the minimum height of 5ft 3in. However, the fall-off in volunteers meant that by 1915 the authorities had become less fussy about who they accepted.

The Bantams were held in great public affection but sometimes praise could be a little patronising. This is how Bristol And The Great War, a book published in 1920, described them: 'They [the Bantams] were a remarkably intelligent and smart lot of men, and they rapidly picked up the rudiments of military discipline and science. The citizens of Bristol took a great interest in the battalion, who were always sure of a hearty reception when they marched through the streets.'

Any suggestion that the Bantams were just grown-up children was set straight by a tale of extraordinary courage from the Front, which was relayed by the *Frenchay Parish Magazine*. Captain Hugh Kinred, a soldier of the 14/Gloucesters and former curate of the parish, was walking along a trench when he saw a bomb drop near seven soldiers who were fast asleep. 'In a moment I saw the danger they were in and that no time could be lost in picking it up: so I decided to smother it by laying on it,' he explained. 'No sooner had I lain on it than it exploded, blowing me from the corner of the trench at an angle of about 30 degrees on to its top, and I should doubtless have been killed but for the lucky chance that I was wearing a Whitfield steel waistcoat [body armour].' Captain Kinred, who sustained serious wounds, was awarded the Military Cross.

* * *

As 1915 drew to a close it was reported by one London newspaper that, despite the war, women were still spending freely as the festive season approached. While shops that depended on male customers were finding business slack, those that attracted women were enjoying record sales. The same was true in Bristol and a look through the local newspapers in the week leading up to Christmas 1915 shows that women had all the encouragement they needed from advertisers.

Alongside a big, bold appeal for army recruits, the pharmacist Henry Hodder, of Wine Street, commanded: 'Do your Xmas shopping now.' The Misses Weymouth of Corn Street offered their furs as ideal yuletide gifts with motor wraps from five guineas and foot muffs at 10s 9d. James Phillips & Sons, a household goods store in Union Street, helpfully let it be known that 'You cannot do better than inspect our large and choice assorted stock of goods'.

In Clifton, the Alexandra Company proudly advertised its dainty fancy goods, while in Augustine's Parade, MW Dunscombe Ltd showed off its Meccano for boys, and suggested their electric torches and pocket Kodaks were a most acceptable present for soldiers at the Front.

Who could blame women for indulging in a bit of retail therapy? They were the ones who were left to bring up families by themselves, who

struggled when food and money was short, and who could not forget that
their loved ones might never return.

**The *Bristol Times and Mirror* advertises some tempting treats for
Christmas 1915.** *[BRL]*

Chapter Three

1916 – The Long Haul

'Take trouble in the kitchen!' was the advice to women.

'IT IS NO USE "keeping yourself going" with incessant cups of
tea and cake, and doing without nourishing food. You must think
of the future; and see to it that you are built up, even if it entails
a little more trouble and thought in the kitchen.'

This was the stern but well-meant advice handed out by the *Bristol Times
and Mirror* to one of the most overlooked sections of Great War society
– the women who stayed at home to take care of their families. When
husbands, brothers and sons went off to fight, the responsibility for the
household fell entirely on their shoulders. Cooking, cleaning, shopping,
paying the bills and looking after the children was a full-time job with
little reward, and it was made all the more difficult by the ever-present
fear that loved ones may never return.

Mothers were now the pillar of many families and, as the *Bristol Times and Mirror* was at pains to point out, it was important to eat well and stay strong: 'It does take a little time and trouble to think about the saving of bones, liquor and fat and so on, but what of that compared with wretched health, delicate children and unpaid butcher's bills through waste and buying unsuitable meat?' wrote the women's page columnist.

At least advice was being tailored to reality. The previous year columns were still being written about the importance of making meals look attractive: 'Few housewives realise the value of garnishes as an asset in the ordinary serving of the daily meals.' By 1916 such matters seemed trivial compared to the far graver concerns that now occupied women's minds. The question now being asked was not when the war would end, but whether it would ever end.

For a second winter, stalemate reigned on the battlefields of Europe and as spring approached, the Allied generals were planning a big push on the Somme that they hoped would break the deadlock. This would be the first major attack to depend on Britain's young volunteers who were now replacing the regular soldiers. The 'old sweats' with years of experience had seen their ranks decimated and many were now either dead or in hospital.

Many regular soldiers were now in hospital, like this trio at Cleve House, Downend. *[FVM]*

The war continued to spread east. After the failure of Gallipoli, the focus had shifted to Mesopotamia where British forces had advanced up the Tigris with the aim of taking Baghdad. But they now found themselves besieged in the town of Kut-al-Amara and would be forced into a humiliating surrender by the Turks. At sea, the Battle of Jutland would claim many Bristol lives when the mighty British Navy took on the German High Seas Fleet in the North Sea in May.

Meanwhile the supply of new recruits at home was drying up and with casualties so high, the government was left with no choice but to introduce conscription in early 1916. Initially only single men between the ages of 18 and 41 were called up, unless they were widowed with children or ministers of religion, but later in the year married men would also be liable and by the end of the war the age limit had been raised to 51.

Enthusiastic volunteers were now harder to find in Bristol, but there were exceptions. One of them was Mr W. J. Davey, whose attempts to enlist in November 1915 were rejected because he only had one leg (the other had been lost in the Boer War). *The Bristol Observer* reported that Mr Davey was so incensed that he took his protest all the way to the King, but to no avail. The authorities did, however, find him work at the Shirehampton Remount Depot.

* * *

With a change in the social order at home, some women faced problems that ran far deeper than anything that could be solved by newspaper advice on healthy eating. For the first time, they were in charge not only of their families but the purse strings too, and for some that proved too much of a temptation. One Easton mother appeared at Bristol Police Court accused of neglecting her three daughters aged 6, 4 and 3. The court heard that each week she received a separation allowance (which the government paid to the wives of serving soldiers), a relief payment from a charitable organisation, plus four shillings that her husband, a sapper with the Royal Engineers, allowed her from his pay. Practically all of it went on drink, the court was told.

A similar story was related by Clifton's Maude Boucher in her wartime journal. When checking the women who had claimed relief payments from the local branch of the Soldiers' and Sailors' Families Association, she noted: 'One woman seemed to be alright, but another we found had gone off to the Hippodrome Music Hall and taken her family with her, and the third woman was dreadful, and we thought she was intoxicated.'

It was a problem that affected the whole country and the War Office was concerned enough to suggest that police should keep an eye on women who were drawing separation allowance. The army paymaster swiftly objected, saying: 'Men at the front will not relish this insult to the women they have left behind.'

Even when there was plenty of money in the kitty, shortages and rising prices meant that it often didn't go very far. Britain had always relied on imported food but when German submarines started targeting merchant shipping, the supply was disrupted and in 1917 food rationing was introduced. Flour was in particularly short supply and there were

Digging allotments at Fishponds.

prosecutions for gross and wilful waste of bread. Sugar was even harder to obtain and in one incident the police were called when women stormed Bristol grocers' shops in search of it. New rules limited the type of pastries and cakes that could be sold, but when government officials began checking up on the city's hotels, shops and restaurants they were greeted by a mouthwatering breach of regulations. 'Puff goods of all kinds, Banbury and Eccles cakes, cheese-cakes, jam turnovers and sausage rolls are all under the ban,' reported one local newspaper, 'yet the official saw in Bristol most tempting things of all kinds, particularly was his attention drawn to some very jammy jam turnovers.'

Everyone was expected to do their bit to ensure there was enough food to go around. Allotments became very popular, householders were encouraged to grow vegetables in their gardens and some householders

began keeping livestock too, perhaps even making a few pennies for themselves. This item appeared in the Frenchay church magazine under the heading Make Your Poultry Pay:

> 'All persons who keep poultry or would like to do so are invited to come to the Village Hall, Frenchay, on Wednesday 1 March, at 3.45 pm, to hear an address on keeping poultry for profit. It is purposed to form a co-operative society for the better production of poultry and eggs, and it is hoped that the meeting will be largely attended.'

The countryside around Bristol played an important part in keeping the city supplied during the war. Milk, cheese, and hay for the horses was brought in from surrounding farms. And when village schoolchildren were given a half-day holiday to pick blackberries an impressive seven tons were collected by the youngsters of Olveston, Pilning, Almondsbury, Northwick and Henbury. The fruit was sent to Bristol by rail and used to make jam for soldiers and sailors.

It wasn't only foodstuffs that were scarce, so too was petrol because of the enormous quantities needed for military and aviation purposes. This led to one of the more unusual sights and sounds in Bristol during the war – buses with gas bags on their roofs. Conventional vehicles were converted so that they could be driven by coal gas. The fuel was stored in a bag made of gas-proof fabric and was reasonably successful as a source of power, although there was one problem: 'The back-firing could not be prevented, and it was a common thing on the journey to hear a series of loud reports like those proceeding from machine-gunfire,' according to *Bristol And The Great War*.

* * *

Security was the number one priority in every British town and city, and everyday life was profoundly affected by the Defence of the Realm Act (better known as DORA), which allowed the government to prosecute anyone whose actions were deemed to 'jeopardise the success of the operations of His Majesty's forces or to assist the enemy'. The Act came into force in August 1914 and as the war progressed, new restrictions were added that covered every possible detail of life. Some were predictable, like press censorship; others less so, like the ban on loitering near bridges and tunnels, or whistling for taxis in case it was mistaken for an air raid siren.

Tucked away in south-west England, Bristol was never attacked by German Zeppelin airships, unlike other parts of the country, but no chances were taken and blackouts were still imposed at night. In the summer of 1916 a tightening of restrictions caught out many Bristolians who had failed to close their curtains properly and on one day alone seventy-five summonses were heard against people for contravening the regulations.

The blackout cast gloom on the streets in winter when two-thirds of the streetlights were turned off. As a result some retailers started shutting up shop early and the city mayor had to appeal to them to extend their hours again, closing at 9 pm on Saturday and 7 pm on all other days except the selected half-day.

Trams also had to have their curtains drawn at night, and motor cars were allowed only their lamps, not headlights, which meant little light was cast on the road ahead. This was all too much for one Bristol motorist who wrote to the *Evening Times and Echo*: 'Whilst driving my car from Kingswood to the city on Sunday night, I received one of the worst shocks to my nerves I have experienced. The night, you will remember, was wet and very dark, so dark that with the small lights we are now permitted, it was impossible to travel at anything but a slow pace, which was fortunate for me.'

As he approached the Lawrence Hill Bridge the correspondent almost crashed into an unlit tram standard in the middle of the road. 'I missed it by inches only, and my car skidded almost into the shop windows on the other side. This is a grave danger to all users of the road which exists in numerous parts of the city.'

DORA allowed the government to rein in the British penchant for drinking which, it was feared, was causing too many days of lost production. Pub opening hours were reduced, beer was made weaker, and the buying of rounds – or 'treating' as it was known – was prohibited.

Away from smoky bars, farmers had their working days extended by the introduction of British Summer Time in May 1916. Fodder for horses was now much in demand from surrounding farms and, for the first time ever, hay was harvested on the Clifton Downs. The sweet smell must have been wonderful for walkers on a warm summer evening.

The war dealt a blow to sports fans when, in 1915, the Football Association bowed to public pressure and halted its national league competition. The move pleased those who believed that men who were fit enough to play football for a living should be fighting for their country.

It was business as usual for White's of Ashton Gate, but the blackout tempted some shops to close early.   *[Wadsworth Family]*

Wagons laden with hay arrive at Chipping Sodbury Station bound for Bristol. *[Y&DHC]*

Professional clubs were now limited to playing in regional wartime leagues or friendly matches that offered lesser opposition. Both Bristol City and Bristol Rovers were affected and many fans were displeased: 'It is hardly worthwhile going down there just to see friendly matches,' complained City fan Alfred Ford of Stapleton in a letter he wrote from the trenches to his brother Fred. 'Give me a good cup tie.'

Compared to clubs in other parts of the country, Bristol City players

had been in no rush to join up. Their star international Billy Wedlock did try, but he was turned down on account of his flat feet. The Ball brothers were more successful, however, and soon found themselves in uniform. Henry, Bert and Fred had grown up next to City's ground at Ashton Gate at the Cooper's Arms pub, which was run by their father Harry.

They all played for City, largely in the smaller competitions, although Henry, the oldest, made a few forays into the first team before the war. And Bert had obvious ambitions when he proudly listed himself as 'profesional footballer' [*sic*] in the 1911 Census. Whether he or his brothers could have gone on to greater things had war not intervened will never be known. They all survived the conflict but their names never appeared on the team sheets again. Henry went into the grocery business, Fred became a caretaker at the coroner's court, but tragically Bert died of tuberculosis in 1923 at the age of 34, leaving behind a wife and five children. It was left to the brothers' young sister, Lillian Ida, to continue the family's footballing tradition by marrying City captain Walter Wadsworth when he arrived at the club in 1926.

Professional football may have been put on hold, but the amateur game continued to flourish and men who had played for their local sides before the war formed new teams when they joined up. There was great enthusiasm for matches at the Front and soldiers looked forward to games

The Ball brothers outside the Cooper's Arms with their parents and sister, from left: Henry, Bert and Fred.   *[Wadsworth Family]*

in their time away from the trenches: 'I see you are doing well off of half-back and I hope you keep it up,' wrote 18-year-old infantryman Fred Wood, of Easton, to his brother Edwin while both were serving in France. Edwin had played for Newtown Rovers before the war.

Service teams at home were also keen to play and in Bristol they provided City and Rovers with plenty of matches. Sides included the Remount League from Shirehampton, the Tractor Depot from Avonmouth, the Bristol Dockers, the Royal Flying Corps from Filton, and Bristol University's Officer Cadets. Most would offer little opposition to the two clubs, although the Royal Engineers based at the White City barracks were tough to beat – unless work got in the way: 'Given as they had been working since the small hours, it was hardly surprising that the Royal Engineers failed to show any of their normal vim and dash,' wrote one understanding reporter when they were beaten by City.

Some matches were played to raise money for various war funds, but most did not attract big crowds and the clubs' attendance dropped dramatically as the war progressed. During the 1917-18 season Bristol City's average gate was no more 650, compared to 10,711 during 1913-14. Numbers were often so paltry that they were not even recorded in figures. Against the Tractor Depot in November 1916, for example, attendance was 'wretched'; versus the Officer Cadets a month later, 'counted on fingers'; and against the Royal Army Service Corps (Avonmouth) in April 1917, 'minuscule'. In fact, according to one local press report: 'The attendance was such that is was likely exceeded by the Depot Band, who discoursed [sic] sweet music before the kick-off.'

Inspired by the freedom that life during the war was giving them, many women loosened their corsets and began playing football too. The game was particularly popular among factory workers who formed their own sides and took each other on in keenly fought matches. Records show that there were female teams at the National Smelting Company and Chittening Gas Factory down at Avonmouth.

And over at Easton young ladies who worked for the engineering company Brecknell, Monro and Rogers were positively encouraged to abandon their inhibitions by taking part in the firm's sports day. The event was held at Bristol Rovers' Eastville ground and included running races, the long jump and a tug o' war competition for women as well as men.

* * *

As more and more men departed for war, Bristol women were now taking

**Women abandoned their inhibitions at Brecknell, Monro and Rogers'
sports day.** *[Jack Williams]*

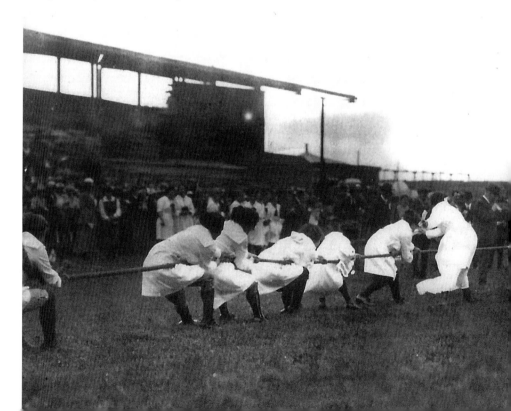

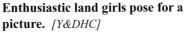

Enthusiastic land girls pose for a picture. *[Y&DHC]*

on new roles with enthusiasm. Large numbers were recruited for the Land Army and although many had been working in dairies, keeping poultry and helping at harvest-time for generations, the less-experienced girls were thoroughly checked to make sure they would 'stick at it'. They had to supply three character references and were then interviewed by a panel. Selection boards were held in the city once a week at the Victoria Street Exchange and some 1,400 women applied in total, of whom about 660 were accepted. It was impressed upon

Proud in her new uniform, firewoman Florence Gough.
[Wood Family]

the successful candidates that although they would be wearing smocks and breeches, they were still expected to behave like ladies. For some, however, the freedom of being billeted on farms unchaperoned was too much of a temptation and many a boisterous night was spent at the local pub.

Some girls were already in jobs when war broke out, especially those from the working classes. Teenager Florence Gough worked at the Wills factory in Bedminster packing cigarettes, where she amused herself by picking up handfuls of exactly twenty with her eyes shut. Had she been born into a later generation she would have gone to college or perhaps university, but there was a limit to what girls from St George could expect from life, so they took their opportunities where they could. Florence's came when Wills needed women for the company's fire-fighting service to replace men who had gone to fight. She was thrilled to be accepted and wore her uniform with pride.

Despite the prominent part women were now playing, many citizens were still more comfortable to see them in supporting, decorative or even subservient roles. Frenchay's parish magazine, which was largely written by the rector, revealed an almost aggressive satisfaction in reporting that nurses at Cleve Hill Hospital in Downend were scrubbing kitchen floors, cleaning sinks, cooking for nearly one hundred people, and washing filthy bandages and dressings. 'It is work that anyone may be proud and thankful to do,' declared the magazine, continuing in Churchillian style: 'For there will come the day when those who limped in can march out, when all bandages and slings can be cast off ... these men will leave England again for the battlefield, and those Red Cross members who sewed and scrubbed and scraped and fetched and carried for them, and nursed them back into health, will know that they have had a finger in the pie which feeds the British Army.'

Similar epic language was used by another Bristol clergyman, who believed it was the duty of women to marry soldiers who were maimed and wounded. The Reverend Ernest Haughton, rector of the city centre parish of St Stephen's, expressed his views in a letter to the local press:

> 'The possibility that a man who has freely offered himself for
> his country and has no alternative but to spend his broken life in
> grim untended loneliness or the grey depression of an institution
> is not to be tolerated ... Maybe many noble-minded patriotic
> women will gladly give their lives and strength to ameliorate the
> conditions of such men.'

Haughton was supported by Dr Meaburn Staniland, a consulting

Red Cross nurses at Cleve House, 'sewing, scrubbing and scraping for the British Army'. *[FVM]*

physician, and fellow clergyman Father F. Shellard, and the trio planned to set up a committee to bring couples together. No names would be divulged, they promised, 'until there seems some probability of arrangement.' The men admitted that pecuniary problems could create hardship in some marriages, but suggested that these could be overcome

if women were given the vote and received equal pay.

Quite how many supported the idea is not known, but the Bishop of Bristol did not. He opposed the scheme and as a result it was abandoned.

The majority of men probably still believed that women should stick to what they did best – looking lovely. And for those who remained at home, what better than a show at the Bristol Hippodrome called The Brilliant British Burlesque Beauties, which promised a pageant of beauty queens from all over the world. 'Miss Japan, Miss Italy, Miss India, Miss America,' gushed one advertisement, 'but NOT Miss Germany!'

* * *

Couples who had still not been separated by war in 1916 did their best to carry on with normal family life. The shops, theatres, churches and parks of Bristol were all still open. So too were the schools, and at Hambrook Evangelical School, on the city's northern edge, headmaster Levi Luff kept a daily log throughout the war years. There were the usual absences through illness (including scarlet fever) and closures due to bad weather: 'A blizzard was raging this am. Only twenty-three [out of nearly 200] children presented themselves and these had such wet feet that I sent them home at once'.

There was praise for the school's garden and religious instruction ('The children are evidently taught in a reverent and conscientious manner') and the usual matters of discipline were commented upon: 'I have had to cane a boy, named Willie Adams, for writing filthy words on a slip of paper and passing it round the class. I gave him three strokes with a small cane, two on one hand and one on the other and warned him that the

The...

Brilliant British Burlesque

BEAUTIES

INTRODUCING:

Miss SCOTLAND
Miss IRELAND
Miss COLONIES
Miss INDIA

Miss FRANCE
Miss BELGIUM
Miss RUSSIA
Miss SERBIA

Miss JAPAN
Miss HOLLAND
Miss ITALY
Miss AMERICA

but not Miss GERMANY

ALLIED BEAUTY CHORUS

FOR FULL COMPANY
SEE PAGE 1.

:: BRISTOL ::

Hippodrome

6.40 and 8.50

THE DISTINCTIVE THEATRE

TELEPHONE   4342   4343

COAL EXPORTS.

AN OFFICIAL EXPLANATION.

The Press Bureau last night issued the following:

Much unnecessary apprehension appears to have been caused by the publication in the supplement to the London Gazette of the 30th July of an Order in Council to the effect that on and after the 14th day of August 1915 the exportation of coal, including anthracite and steam, gas, household and all other kinds of coal and coke, would be prohibited to all destinations abroad other than British possessions and protectorates. The Secretary of State for Foreign Affairs desires to explain that this regulation is in itself in no way intended to alter the actual state of affairs with regard to the export of coal beyond the fact that licences will be required for coal exported to any place which is not a British possession or protectorate. The Order is not designated for the purpose of entirely preventing coal exports, but is the consequence of certain domestic legislation by which the price of coal in the United...

Burlesque Beauties advertised in the *Bristol Times and Mirror*.   [BRL]

punishment would be doubled if he ever repeated the offence.'

Meanwhile, at the altogether grander Clifton College older boys were expressing their own opinions in the school magazine *The Cliftonian*. 'As the National Anthem has been introduced into the Chapel Service, it is surely obvious that the school should be allowed to sing it. If it is necessary for the choir to sing some part solo let it be the second verse, which could then be omitted,' suggested one lad who obviously preferred the sound of his own voice to that of the choir.

For many families, this would be their final year together. Now that married men were liable for conscription husbands had no choice but to enlist, although the thought of their wives struggling at home alone was hard for many to bear.

Soldiers like Private Tom Fake, a carpenter from Horfield, sent frequent letters to his wife Charlotte when he was posted to France. Money was a particular concern: 'I should have sent you some more cash, but I have had only one pay since I sent you last, and shall not be having another for about another fortnight,' he wrote apologetically. To make ends meet she took in soldiers' shirts to sew, but this was met with a cautious response: 'I say my dear, you have got a lot of shirts to get on with, I do hope you will not overdo it and make yourself ill again this winter.'

A neighbour had also taken in army sewing but it seems her husband, who was serving alongside Tom Fake, was rather sensitive about it: 'I shall not say anything to him about the shirt-making for it is quite likely he may not like to think of anyone else knowing that she does it,' wrote Fake.

When the lodgers to whom Charlotte rented out rooms became difficult, her husband could barely contain his frustration at not being at home to sort things out: 'I don't like to see you put upon like this, it's a rotten shame and if he is like you say, you must put your foot on it at once ... Now there are two ways of getting about it. One is to see a stipendiary magistrate and explain everything to him and ask him what he can do for you. Another way is to go to the Soldiers' and Sailors' Families Association and get them to do it for you, but they must go now they are carrying on this foolery.' The unwelcome guests eventually left.

Private Fake's correspondence is particularly poignant when he writes about his 7-year-son, Tommy, whom he is obviously missing. These snippets are from letters written from the trenches in 1917:

26 May: 'I am wishing Tommy many happy returns of his birthday. I am sorry I cannot send him a present but am enclosing a couple of flowers I picked just over a week ago.'

4 June: 'Thank Tommy for his nice letter and tell him my next letter will be to him. I am also glad he has had a bible as a prize from his Sunday school and I hope he will take care of it.'

25 June: 'He has some funny ideas of girls, he says they are made of sugar and spice and all that's nice, starting young ain't he?'

6 September: 'So Tommy thinks he's a man now with his new hat. I think it will be nice to get him a rainproof coat, and as you

Private Tom Fake with wife Charlotte and son Tommy. *[Jackie Carpenter]*

say if it's plenty big enough it will do for a second season.'

2 October: 'I am sorry Tommy worries about me like he do, I wish he wouldn't but still, we are all of the same breed, I am just longing for the time to come, but we must have patience.'

* * *

Tom Fake landed in France with the Rifle Brigade in December 1916, just as the Battle of the Somme had drawn to a close. The offensive had been launched in July and was intended to give the Allies a decisive breakthrough after two years of stalemate in the trenches. The generals who planned the attack believed the Germans would offer little resistance, but on the first day alone, line after line of Tommies advanced across No Man's Land only to be mown down by machine guns or blown to bits by shells. It was a baptism of fire for the raw recruits of Kitchener's Army, and by mid-November, Britain had suffered more than 420,000 casualties and little ground had been gained.

One man more than any other has been held responsible for the indiscriminate slaughter on the Somme, the commander of the British Army in France, Field Marshal Douglas Haig. As an officer he would have braced himself for the controversy his tough policies provoked, but it was something he could hardly have envisaged when he arrived in Bristol some forty years earlier to begin his first term at Clifton College.

Haig was one of two Cliftonians who would rise to prominence in the Great War, the other was Field Marshal William Birdwood, commander of Australian and New Zealand troops (the Anzacs) in the Dardanelles and later Europe. As characters the two men couldn't have been more different. While Haig was regarded by many as aloof and private, Birdwood was a genial man whose down-to-earth manner earned him the respect of the Anzacs – something they didn't give easily. The men's schooldays give a fascinating insight into the people they would become.

Both arrived at Clifton College in 1877, although at the age of 14 Haig was four years older. Birdwood recalled spending 'five happy years' at Clifton. 'I usually kept a steady place near the bottom of whatever form I happened to be in,' he wrote in his autobiography. 'But I was a keen member of our Cadet Corps ... We did practical bridge-making, pontooning, and so forth, in the lake at the Clifton Zoological Gardens – exercise that provides fine opportunities for "ducking". I was a poor cricketer, but I dearly loved rugby football, the school runs, and swimming, for which I won many prizes.' His school reports reflected an easygoing attitude: 'Idle/not v. strenuous', 'Not quite sat [satisfactory] but better than last term', 'Hopeful, must take great pains', 'Conduct v.g.'.

On leaving school, Birdwood's housemaster was doubtful that he would get into the army's officer training college at Sandhurst quickly: 'It is not likely he will succeed very early, perhaps not for two years.' However, Birdwood proved him wrong and was successful at his first attempt although he was typically modest about this achievement: 'Somewhat to my surprise I succeeded in passing it – though very low down on the list.'

Birdwood grew up in India, where his father was under-secretary to the Government of Bombay; in contrast, Haig was born in Scotland where his family was more concerned with commerce than empire. He was the eleventh and

Field Marshal William Birdwood: 'Hopeful, must take great pains'.

youngest child of John Haig, head of the famous whisky distilling company. As a boy he suffered badly from asthma and possibly for this reason started at Clifton later than most. At times he struggled academically but he worked hard, encouraged by the mother he adored, and managed to come top in Latin in his final year. Haig was generous in his praise of the master who had tutored him so well: 'I had a very affectionate regard for our friend Dakyns [H.G. Dakyns, one of the classic masters], and if I took interest in Ovid, it was entirely owing to his personality and good taste, which threw a sort of reflected light on to me as one of his pupils,' he wrote to a friend.

Haig was an excellent sportsman and played rugby for the college. He also represented his form on the school's Big-Side Levée, a committee that organised sporting competitions. However, contemporary accounts make him a hard figure to pin down. 'A quiet, determined youngster,' was one master's description, 'honest and straightforward' was another. A fellow pupil said he was 'popular, nice-looking, and seemed to do everything gracefully and without any effort'. Another remembered him as taciturn in class and, when asked if he noticed any signs of future eminence, the boy replied: 'I can't say I did.'

Clifton College had always supplied the services with a steady stream of officers, and at the outbreak of war some eighty old boys were already in the Royal Navy and 700 (including Haig and Birdwood) were in the British Army. By the end of the war a total of 3,100 Cliftonians had served on land, sea and in the air, of whom 578 were dead. To put it more poignantly, of the college's 1914 first Cricket XI, five had been killed, one died of disease, and four were wounded.

Field Marshal Douglas Haig: 'Honest and straightforward'.

* * *

'Casualties comparatively light' reported the *Western Daily Press* following the launch of the Somme offensive. 'Fearless advance into a bath of lead', trumpeted the *Bristol Times and Mirror*. In fairness, it was probably difficult for newspaper correspondents to learn exactly what was happening amid the chaos of the Somme battlefield, and the government certainly would not have wanted to hand out damning information. But on the first day alone, the British had sustained almost 60,000 casualties. The truth began filtering through when, day after day, long lists of the dead, wounded, missing and those taken prisoner began appearing in the papers.

There was, however, some cause for cheer when the 14/Gloucesters – better known as the diminutive Bristol Bantams – captured a German machine gun during a raid on enemy trenches at Neuve Chapelle. It was

The Bantams' captured machine gun goes on display at Bristol Museum, a sketch by Samuel Loxton. *[BRL, Ref N1023]*

sent home and put on show at the city museum for all to see.

The Battle of the Somme lasted from July to November 1916 and survivors who arrived home on leave in December were grateful to be alive. Maude Boucher pasted a newspaper cutting into her scrapbook, which described the happy and busy scenes at Temple Meads Station:

> 'All day the station was crowded with soldiers, coming and going and changing trains. The Christmas spirit was noisily evident, and the singing of snatches of songs, continuous. Never, surely, were trains more crowded, never were travellers more good humoured and content with their accommodation. The men got into the trains anyhow – some through the windows. They did not ask guards or porters to find them seats, but jumped into any compartment, not caring a toss whether they could sit or not ... They did not mind so long as they got aboard and knew that they were going home.'

Sadly, Maude Boucher's brother was not among them. Captain Frank Hannam of the 4th Battalion, The Gloucestershire Regiment, husband of Edith, a former pupil of Bristol Grammar School, captain of Bristol Rugby Club, and president of Bristol Cricket Association and the Gloucestershire Rugby Union, had been killed on the Somme.

Chapter Four

1917 – The City Rolls Up Its Sleeves

Wrapped up against the cold, King George at the investiture on Durdham Downs. *[Bristol and the Great War, Wells and Stone, 1920]*

A ROYAL VISIT was just what was needed to raise spirits in 1917 and crowds turned out in their thousands when King George V and Queen Mary came to see the city at work that November. The day was bitterly cold, although thankfully fine, and the couple were warmly dressed as they stepped from the royal train on to the platform at Temple Meads Station to shake hands with the long line of dignitaries. The queen wore

Royal visitors King George V and Queen Mary won the admiration of Bristolians.

a long dark gown with a fur wrap around her shoulders, and a tall hat trimmed with feathers; the king was dressed in military uniform, with shining spurs attached to his boots and a warm greatcoat.

Their itinerary would take them to the National Shell Factory at St Philip's, the Wills cigarette factory in Bedminster and, after a break for lunch on the royal train followed by an investiture ceremony on the Downs, on to the British and Colonial Aircraft Company's workshops at Filton. The royal party would spend the night aboard the train at a quiet siding at Henbury before moving on to Bath and Wiltshire the next day.

Newly married Florence Cottle, who lived at Easton with her mother, described the occasion (with a few wistful thoughts of her own) in a letter to her husband who was fighting in France: 'There was a bit of excitement yesterday as the king and queen came here, they say the town was packed but I didn't go to see him. If it had been my own king I would of [*sic*] run a mile, but the day is still coming darling to our meeting.' Florence had tried, without much luck, to catch a glimpse of the royals from a neighbour's house: 'The train went through by us so Mother said come round Mrs Rogers' as we could see out in her garden. Mother went on and was only just in time, I missed him by a minute.'

The royal tour was a very public event, tracked continuously by journalists. This was in stark contrast to a visit the king and queen had made to Bristol two years earlier, to meet wounded soldiers and inspect the remount depot at Shirehampton. By royal request, this visit had been kept as quiet as possible with no announcements made beforehand; even the mayor had received only one week's notice. The secrecy was no doubt for security reasons but perhaps also because the royals were wary about the reception they would receive. The British people were suspicious of anyone who had links with the enemy, and the families of both King George and Queen Mary had German connections. Indeed, the king's first cousin was none other than the German Kaiser Wilhelm II himself. To make matters worse, the royal family name, inherited from Queen Victoria's husband Prince Albert, was the Germanic-sounding Saxe-Coburg and Gotha.

Despite the secrecy, news of the 1915 visit still got out and thousands of people watched the royal procession go by – happily without incident. By 1917 King George had changed his family name to the more English-sounding Windsor, and few now doubted where his loyalties lay. When their visit ended the king and the queen had won the admiration of Bristolians with their down-to-earth concern for those they met, showing 'a real fellow feeling in their people's efforts and sacrifices'.

* * *

The factories visited by the royal couple in 1917 were just the tip of the iceberg when it came to Bristol's contribution to the First World War. The city had long been noted for the diversity of its manufacturing and commerce, and even in times of depression unemployment was never as severe as in cities which were dependent on just one industry. When war broke out Bristol was producing everything from cotton, leather and soap to paper bags, chocolate and boots, and this would be the foundation for the huge range of goods the city sent to the Front.

Now in its fourth year, the war of attrition in Europe with its voracious demand for men and munitions showed no sign of ending. The conflict had become increasingly sophisticated with tanks, aircraft, gas, heavy artillery and machine guns all now an accepted part of the fighting. In 1917 a series of big attacks would be launched on the Western Front, beginning in spring with the Battle of Arras and winding up with the Battles of Passchendaele and Cambrai that winter. Despite huge numbers of casualties none of these battles was decisive enough for victory.

Businesses all over Britain were keen to do their patriotic duty and Bristol had been particularly inspired to do so when David Lloyd George made a flying visit in 1915. Lloyd George, who would later become prime minister, had just been put in charge of the new Ministry of Munitions, which was set up to deal with shell shortages on the battlefield. In this role he was a brilliant success, travelling up and down the country to talk to businessmen about how they could help.

David Lloyd George.

When Lloyd George arrived at Stapleton Road Station he was cheered by crowds as he hurried into a cab to keep an appointment at the Council House. There he met the bosses of local engineering firms and munitions producers and encouraged them to adapt their production to meet the needs of war. It was something they were only too willing to do.

For example, soap had always been the main product of Christopher Thomas and Brothers Ltd at its Broad Plain Soap Works, and glycerine was simply a by-product. In 1915 the government requisitioned the company's glycerine production to make explosive propellants, which were needed to fire shells from guns and bullets from rifles. As a result,

A paparazzi-style shot of David Lloyd George arriving at Stapleton Road Station in 1915.

Broad Plain worked day and night to provide glycerine for the war and soap became the by-product.

On the banks of the Feeder Canal at St Philip's, the engineering company John Lysaght Ltd had long served the farming community with goods such as wire mesh fencing, sheep feeders and cattle troughs. The demands of war meant that it now began producing barbed wire and wire netting for the battlefields, Nissen huts and steel sheds for aeroplanes and motor transport. Lysaght's was also one of many companies that began manufacturing much-needed shell cases for the War Office. Another was Brecknell, Munro and Rogers of Easton, where they were made in a converted Baptist chapel in Thrissell Street. Brecknell's had brought the empty premises for £650 in 1880, when the church moved to the new Kensington Chapel in Stapleton Road. Since then it had been used to store engineering machinery but it found new life as a munitions factory where women made up a large part of the workforce.

So great was the demand for shell cases that even non-engineering factories found ways to make them. The tobacco manufacturer W.D. and H.O. Wills and chocolate maker J.S. Fry both converted their repair and maintenance workshops for the purpose.

Shell cases from all over the West Country were sent to a big collection centre at Victoria Road in St Philip's to be finished, inspected and accepted. This was the National Shell Factory that the king and queen had visited. During the course of the war the factory's output of 18lb high-explosive shell cases was 3,044,337. A further 169,673 18lb shrapnel shell cases were rectified, with cast iron sockets replaced by brass.

* * *

It wasn't just combat equipment that Bristol supplied. The city also became well-known for providing treats for the troops – namely chocolate and cigarettes. J.S. Fry and Sons, one of the city's largest and oldest employers, shipped cocoa and chocolate to servicemen all over the world – France, Salonika, Russia, Mesopotamia and Africa – as well as to army camps at home, naval depots and to prisoners of war. The total tonnage equated to millions of bars of chocolate.

Smaller chocolate firms like H.J. Packer of Greenbank, Carsons of Shortwood and Weber's of Fishponds also contributed to the war effort. At Christmas 1914 the city had held a Chocolate Day when festively

Workers at Brecknell, Monro and Rogers manufacturing shell cases, opposite and overleaf. *[Jack Williams]*

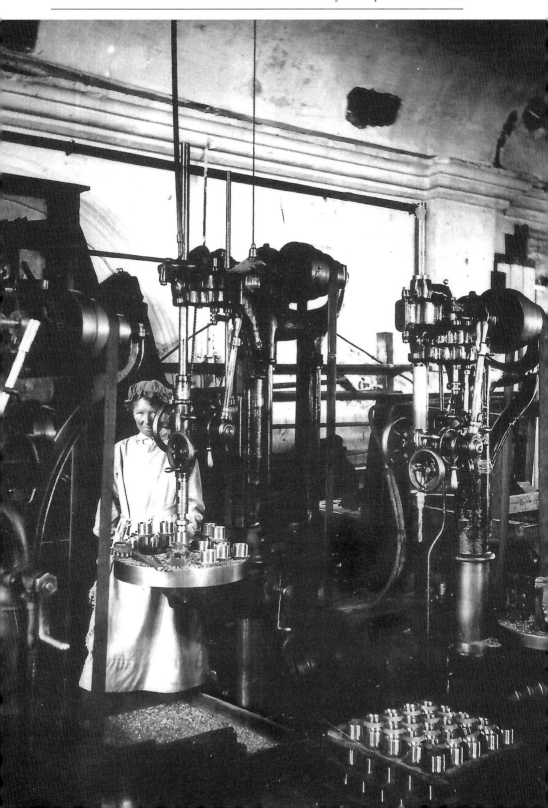

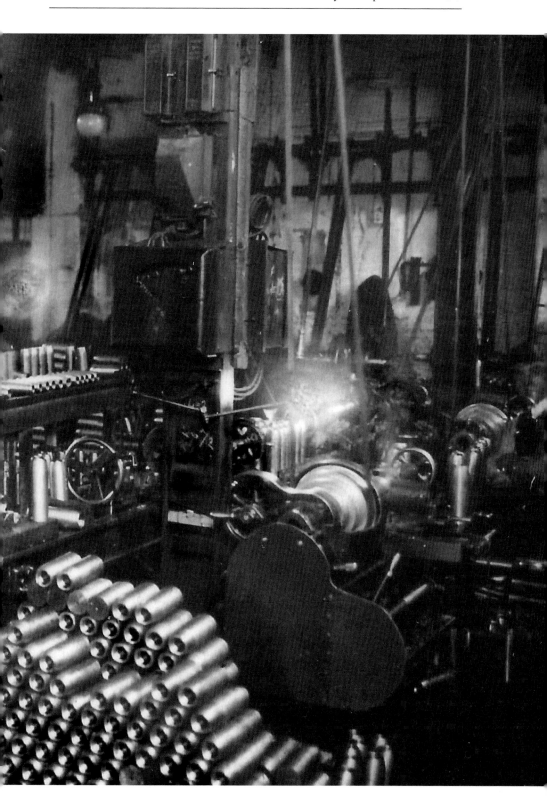

Women made up a large proportion of the workforce at Brecknell, Monro and Rogers. *[Jack Williams]*

packaged chocolate was put on sale at grocers, confectioners, theatres and picture houses for people to buy and donate to soldiers and sailors. Seven tons of chocolate were bought.

Cigarettes were perhaps more of a necessity than a treat for many soldiers and few letters were sent home that did not include a request for them. 'Send as many smokes as you like Dad, they will be very

acceptable' wrote Signaller Edwin Wood of Easton when his battalion had crossed the Alps into Italy in December 1917. W.D. and H.O. Wills would send millions of cigarettes to the Front, along with thousands of pounds of tobacco and hundreds of thousands of cigars. The same was true of the British-American Tobacco Company, which owned a large factory at Ashton Gate.

The British-American Tobacco Company produced weekly wartime

THE
SUNSHINE MOB
Resting
Aprés les Trenches.

'Send as many smokes as you like' wrote Edwin Wood sitting on the right.
Note that three of the five soldiers have cigarettes in their hands.
[Wood Family]

bulletins that kept its employees, and those of associated companies, in touch. When the conflict ended the pages were filled with news of men who were at last on their way home, but one sad item stood out in the edition of 20 September 1919. Edged with a black border it read:

> 'The regrettable news has reached us that Private A.G. Chappell, missing as from April 11, 1918, is now officially reported to have fallen. Born June 16 1899, he entered the service of the Company in June 1913, where he was deservedly popular among his fellow workers.'

Alfred Chappell, aged 18, came from Bedminster where he lived with his parents, brothers and sisters. He began work at Wills at the age of 14, maybe as an apprentice, and had probably expected to be there for life.

The sad report of Alfred Chappell's death
[Christine Lillington]

Wills and Fry's were among many patriotic employers who kept jobs open for their workers after the war. Those who were able also paid allowances to top up employees' service pay, like Ferris and Co, a pharmaceutical chemist in Union Street that was run by Maude Boucher's husband Charles. In her wartime scrapbook she wrote:

'Several of the men from Ferris's went to the war, and by degrees, the number eventually reached thirty. Ferris's did what so many other firms have done, and that was, to make up the men's wages in full all the time they were away, and keep their posts open for them. One of Charlie's principal clerks went and, of course, it gave all those who were left behind a great deal of extra work to do. It could not be helped at such a time as this, and one rarely hears a grumble from anybody.'

* * *

While cigarettes and chocolate bars were busily being dispatched to the battlefields, Bristol was playing its part in the export of something far more sinister on the banks of the Severn Estuary. At a factory at Chittening, north of Avonmouth, mustard gas was being manufactured that would be used against the Germans in the final months of war.

Production began in June 1918 when the government sent thirty chemists to start things off. Within six weeks large quantities of HS gas as it was known (a code that simply stood for Hun Stuff) were being produced.

A few months later the factory appears to have been converted into a more sophisticated plant where not only was gas manufactured but shells were filled too. Officially it was known as National Shell Filling Factory No23, but locals simply called it Chittening Gas Factory. The geometric layout and narrow-gauge railway surrounding the site are visible on old aerial photographs, although it is now built over.

National Shell Filling Factories had sprung up all over the country, with some the size of small villages. All were a safe distance from centres of population and the workforce was largely female. *Bristol and the Great War*, published in 1920, revealed the following about Chittening Gas Factory:

'Shells were filled by a large body of women and girls, who proved just as courageous as the men in sticking to the work,

The effect of German poison gas on British positions.

though there was sometimes quite a considerable number affected
by gas. On one morning there were 140 cases for hospital
treatment, and in all during the period of the work nearly 1,300
persons were more or less seriously gassed.'

The dangers of mustard gas were ever-present. It was capable of causing
huge blisters, blindness and internal bleeding. It also attacked the
bronchial tubes leaving victims fighting for breath.

Workers had to sign an oath of secrecy before employment began and
little was known about exactly what went on inside the factory. However,
the hazards were suggested by notices on the perimeter warning people
not to pick blackberries within a mile of the site in case they were
contaminated. Locals also remarked on a cloying smell, rather like wild
garlic, that hung over the area.

The late Avonmouth historian Ethel Thomas discovered a few of
Chittening's secrets when she interviewed a man called Reginald Tayler,

who had worked there as an errand boy. He recalled an explosion that killed three French scientists in a laboratory and an incident in which workmen had their legs badly burnt when gas leaked into a trench they were digging.

Chittening mustard gas was first used against the Germans on 30 September 1918 – apparently with great success – just a few weeks before the Armistice was signed.

To the south of Chittening one of Bristol's most extraordinary tales of the war unfolded at Hallen in 1917 when a huge explosives factory started to be constructed at a site known as HM Henbury. Thousands of workers were brought in from all over the country and the site was a hive of activity as roads were built, buildings erected and water mains laid.

Then on 8 May, just as quickly as work had begun, the whole project was called off and HM Henbury was abandoned half-finished. The reason? The United States had just entered the war and assured Britain that it could supply nitro-cellulose, which was to have been manufactured there, far more cheaply.

Although abandonment made sense economically, there was still an outcry over the wasted money. In 1919 the government's comptroller and auditor-general estimated that it stood to lose nearly £650,000 (roughly £28,500,000 in today's money), which included payment of compensation to contractors who had been promised orders worth £2,000,000.

* * *

Women were now becoming an increasingly important part of the workforce and were moving into jobs that had once been a strictly male preserve. In 1917 the Bristol Tramways Company decided to employ female conductors, 'clippies' as they were known, to replace men who had gone to fight, and the first batch of twenty-five, smartly dressed in their new uniforms, made a happy photograph for the local press. But smiles would change to strife in 1920 when men demanded their old jobs back.

There was also a proud announcement from Bristol's chief constable when he took on the country's first female detective. Her duties would chiefly concern women and children, he said, although she would play a part in solving all classes of crime and mystery. There was just one concern:

The city's first twenty-five lady tram conductors.
[BRL, Bristol and the War magazine]

'Unfortunately it is sometimes unsafe to trust a woman with an important investigation where young men are concerned. They are swayed by emotion. They can't help it; it is their nature, and they have been known to fall in love with the man they have been set to watch.'

In the early years of war the type of work women undertook was generally divided according to class. The more affluent took on voluntary or hospital work and the lower classes were occupied in factories, as many had been before the war. But as the demand for factory labour grew, pressure increased on ladies from all classes to roll up their sleeves. This was evident when the country's first munitions training centre opened at Bristol North Baths on Gloucester Road. The baths were still being built when the site was handed over and wouldn't be finished until after the war. The aim was to train workers for aircraft construction and those recruited were disabled soldiers and sailors, men rejected by the army – and well-bred ladies.

Ladies from all classes were encouraged to take on factory jobs, like these from the aircraft manufacturer Parnall and Sons.
[Matthew Richardson]

One local newspaper reported:

> 'Young women of superior education are included in the first batch of over 200 who are there, and it is hoped that well-educated and intelligent young women will avail themselves of the opportunity of getting into semi-skilled work. Those who go there will be trained in metal and woodworking,'

Many would go on to work at the British and Colonial Aeroplane Company at Filton, and it was here that one of Bristol's most impressive stories of the war would emerge.

When the conflict began, aeronautics was in its infancy. The first powered flight by humans had been achieved by the American Wright brothers just ten years earlier, and the public were still gasping in amazement at the gravity-defying feats they saw at flying displays. Within a matter of years, however, aircraft were an established part of war and this was due in no small part to Bristol businessman Sir George White.

White was a man with great vision and a fascination for transport. His beginnings were fairly ordinary. Born in 1854 he was the son of a painter and decorator and a lady's maid and grew up at Kingsdown. In his first job as a solicitor's clerk with a law firm in Corn Street, his energy and ability enabled him to rise quickly through the ranks. White was asked to take legal control of the city council's new tram line, which offered the latest in fast and cheap

Sir George White, a man with great vision. *[Airbus]*

transport. Not everyone wanted trams rumbling past their homes though. 'Is it not something terrible and most wicked that the disgusting tramway is to bring the nasty, low inhabitants of Bristol up into our sacred region?' wrote a well-heeled resident of Clifton to the *Bristol Mercury*.

By the time he was 20 White was company secretary of the Bristol Tramway and Carriage Company and later became chairman. He would introduce electric trams, motor buses and motor taxis to the city and was also a sharp operator on Bristol's stock exchange, investing his money first in railways and then aviation – which is where this story begins.

In 1910, White set up the British and Colonial Aeroplane Company (BCAC) in two sheds at Filton. Within a year it had become the world's largest aircraft factory and when war was declared White immediately began supplying the government with planes, which became universally known as Bristols.

Early in the conflict, aircraft were used for battlefield reconnaissance and the Bristol Scout was among the first to perform this task. Built without armament it was up to the aircrew to find ways of defending themselves against enemy aircraft and their methods varied from ramming each other to throwing grenades. As more planes filled the skies, so they

were adapted for combat with mounted machine-guns. At Filton the result was the famous Bristol Fighter, a two-seater aircraft that allowed the pilot to fire a machine gun through the propeller at the front while the observer had another machine-gun to defend against attack from behind.

Aircraft were also being adapted to drop bombs and towards the end of the war the giant, long-range Bristol Triplane was being developed at Filton to attack Berlin from the air. It had four engines and could fly at 125mph carrying 2,700lb of bombs, plus enough water, fuel and oil for a 500-mile trip. This was a huge achievement for the time but the Armistice was signed before the plane could ever be used in anger.

After the war the design was converted into a fourteen-seater passenger plane, complete with plush Pullman fittings, and it caused quite a stir at the 1920 Olympia Air Show in London where nothing as big or luxurious

The Bristol Fighter was built for aerial combat although it seemed of little concern to grazing sheep! *[Airbus]*

Filton's giant Bristol Triplane – the bomber that never was. *[Airbus]*

had been seen before. However, it never operated commercially because its landing speed was considered too fast.

By the final year of the war the BCAC had built more than 4,000 planes for military use and had more than 3,000 people on its payroll, many of them women. Although it was not the only British company designing and building aircraft, it was the most important as far as training pilots was concerned. Before the war George White had set up his own training schools where a large proportion of British First World War aviators learned to fly, although most were far from experienced when they were sent on their first missions.

Sadly Sir George White, who was made a baronet in 1904, did not live long enough to appreciate everything his company achieved. Nor did he witness the formation of the Royal Air Force when the army's Royal Flying Corps and the navy's Royal Naval Air Service merged in 1918. Suffering from ill-health during his final years, he died in November 1916 and was laid to rest with his wife in a vault at St Mary's Church in Stoke Bishop. Although he had asked for a simple funeral the churchyard was full of mourners.

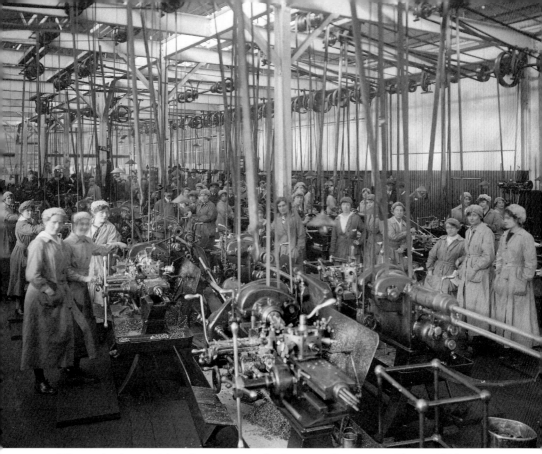

Women in the machine shop and men in the propeller shop at Filton, 1918.
[Airbus]

His company became known simply as the BAC (Bristol Aeroplane Company) and its legacy continues today through giant organisations like Airbus and BAE Systems, which his company spawned. Today Filton is still a centre of the aeronautical industry.

* * *

Despite all the advances, flying was still a hazardous occupation for pilots during the First World War, especially as they didn't carry parachutes. Estimates of life-expectancy at the Front varied considerably but most were measured in days or weeks. The riskiness of it all was brought home to the community of Frenchay in May 1917 when the son of a local headmaster was killed in a flying accident in Kent.

As a child Harry Wadlow had been a pupil at the Frenchay National School,

Harry Wadlow (middle row, right) was a talented sportsman who met a tragic end. *[FVM]*

where his father Henry was still the head. He went on to Bristol Grammar School where he excelled at sport as well as his studies, and when war broke out Harry joined the Army Service Corps. He served in the Dardanelles and France, where he was promoted to captain, then transferred to the Royal Flying Corps in 1916.

The fatal accident happened when he was training to fly a single-seater De Havilland fighter at Joyce Green Aerodrome near Dartford. Situated on marshland, the airfield was not a popular one and Air Vice-Marshal Arthur Stanley Gould Lee, a pilot during the First World War, later explained why:

> 'A pupil taking off with a choked or failing engine had to choose, according to wind direction, between drowning in the Thames [half-a-mile wide at this point], crashing into the Vickers TNT [explosives] Works, sinking into a vast sewage farm, killing himself and numerous patients in a large isolation hospital, being electrocuted in an electrical station with acres of pylons and cables; or trying to turn and get back to the aerodrome. Unfortunately, many pupils confronted with disaster tried the last course and span to their deaths.'

Exactly what happened to Harry is unknown, but he died instantly when his aircraft struck a hut on his landing approach.

The news was broken to his father at morning school and the effect was awful. 'Mr Wadlow was in a terrible state when he got the news and he fell to the ground,' recalled one pupil. It was the second time tragedy had struck, for in 1901 his wife Laura had died, aged 31, of scarlet fever. Harry Wadlow was buried at Frenchay with full military honours in a grave shared with his mother. He was 22 years old.

* * *

In the years leading up to the war Britain had been in the grip of industrial unrest as workers protested over poor conditions, low pay and high prices. In Bristol it was the coal miners and dockers who were among the most militant. When war broke out, strikes were prohibited under the 1915 Munitions of War Act and stoppages declined – at least for the first two years. But as the conflict made more demands on businesses and employees, so discontent began to rear its head again. In December 1917 more than 1,000 aircraft woodworkers in Bristol went on strike to claim the same 12? per cent pay increase, plus five shillings bonus, that had recently been awarded to the engineering trade. The following year 2,000 woodworkers caused serious disruption when they took action in factories at Filton and Brislington.

Bristol's boot and shoe industry was also dogged by stoppages. This had always been a huge employer in the city and at its peak in the 1890s some 129 companies provided work for around 10,000 people. Light footwear was manufactured mainly in the city centre and heavier boots in the eastern suburbs such as Kingswood.

The war brought enormous orders for army boots, not just for British servicemen but for the Allies too, and every firm was called upon to step-up production. Footwear had to be tailored for different theatres of war: mountain boots for the Serbs, high-leg cavalry boots (size: large) for the Russians, sandals for Bedouin tribesmen who fought with the Allies in the desert, and canvas shoes for hospitals. This meant bringing in extra workers and new machines, and discontent on the shop floor often resulted. Despite this, Bristol managed to turn out between three and four million pairs of boots during the war.

Meanwhile manufacturers still had to cater for civilians and when prices in the shops began to soar the government stepped in with a fixed cost for shoes and boots of standard specification. This scheme operated for fifteen months and the sales figures below reflect buying habits that are still familiar today:

Women: 8,285,000 (pairs)

Men: 6,755,000

Boys: 4,585,000

Girls: 3,150,000

Army regiments with Bristol soldiers in their ranks were never short of cobblers and the Gloucesters had plenty like Sergeant Jack House of St George, who would go on to run his own shop, the Boot Box, when the war ended.

The well-known Douglas Motors of Kingswood was another firm that had problems with a disgruntled workforce. In May 1915, 700 walked out when the War Office asked for an increase in the number of motorcycles produced at the factory. Workers felt they should be paid a bonus for the extra work, although bosses insisted they were acting in a patriotic spirit by charging the War Office as little as possible. Terms were eventually agreed and normal production was resumed.

Bristol cobblers like Sergeant Jack House, right, kept the Gloucestershire Regiment well shod.   *[SoGM, Ref: GLRRM: 04531.112]*

Douglas motorcycles were much sought-after at the battlefront and their reliability and resilience was renowned. In all 25,000 of these 'splendid little motor bicycles' (as *Bristol and the Great War* referred to them) were supplied to the army, navy and air force. They were put to work not only at the Western Front but on the tough terrain of lesser-known theatres of war such as Northern Russia, the deserts of Persia and Kurdistan, and on the sweltering, unmade roads of Africa. With few exceptions the motorcycles achieved their objectives with flying colours.

Bristol's contribution to the war could fill a book of its own. Still unmentioned are the factories that turned out clothing for soldiers and sailors; Portishead Dock, which was a major supplier of petrol for transport and aviation in England and France; and Parnall's, which manufactured sea planes for the Admiralty. Its erection workshop at Park Row was in the Coliseum building which had formerly been a roller skating rink.

The First World War also spawned one of the most memorable emblems of Bristol's industry, the zinc-smelting works that once dominated the Avonmouth skyline with its 100-metre chimney. The smelter was opened in 1917 to process lead and zinc residues from ores mined in Australia. Before the conflict these had been processed in Germany and exported to Britain, but when all German contracts were cancelled Britain decided to import the residues itself and built a smelter on the Severn Estuary. The chimney puffing out yellow vapour was a well known landmark for drivers on the M5 until it was demolished in 2003.

* * *

Patriotism was something that varied widely within the population of Bristol. While some were happy to sacrifice their own comforts for the war, others preferred to put themselves first and this was the attitude that pervaded a city centre hostel for munitions workers, where little heed was apparently paid to food shortages that affected the rest of Bristol.

The story came out in May 1917 when Thomas Patterson, who managed the Nimrod Hostel in St Augustine's which housed 400 workers, was summonsed to appear at Bristol police court accused of the gross and wilful waste of bread. Magistrates heard that tubs containing 95lb of bread – chiefly ends of loaves and dry slices – had been put out for collection despite restrictions on such waste. When a tub was presented to the court, magistrates were heard to utter 'shocking'.

The manager insisted that the bread had been put out mistakenly and that he had intended to use it for puddings. Other witnesses told a different story. One female member of staff said the men refused to eat bread pudding and threw it back at her. They did the same with crusts and stamped them on the ground. The local press was outraged: 'Fastidious navvies won't eat crusts or bread puddings!' screamed one headline. Another witness said the navvies were abusive and complained they weren't getting enough to eat despite being allowed more than guests at the Royal Hotel nearby.

An ironic twist to this unsavoury tale was that the discarded bread would never have been discovered if the man contracted to clear the tubs,

Recruits at the central library looked older and more weary than the volunteers of 1914. *[BRL, Ref Z1868, Samuel Loxton]*

a cattle and pig dealer from Horfield, had not been stopped at Stokes Croft for being drunk in charge of a horse and cart as he returned home with his load.

* * *

Bristol's most precious commodity was men and with conscription now in full swing it took a good excuse to get out of fighting. 'Combing out' was the term used for recruiting every last man, and as the need for soldiers became more desperate, those who had once been rejected now found themselves declared fit to serve. A new recruitment office had opened at the central library and the men who presented themselves now looked decidedly older and more weary than the excited volunteers of 1914.

There was a right to appeal against conscription and local tribunals were set up to decide who should or should not be exempted. The chairman of the Bristol Local Tribunal was former mayor John Swaish (later Sir John), although it wasn't a position that endeared him to the customers at his pawnbroker's shop in Lawrence Hill. By 1918, Swaish's

Sir John Swaish, whose position on the conscription tribunal did not endear him to customers. *[Bristol and the Great War, Wells and Stone, 1920]*

tribunal had considered the cases of 22,000 men, of whom 17,000 (three-quarters) were refused exemption.

One of them may have been Private Frederick Hardingham, a 34-year-old widower from Bedminster and the father of three children. Hardingham's wife had died of tuberculosis just before the war and when he was recruited his daughter and two sons were left in the care of relatives. In April 1917 Hardingham found himself in northern France with the 51st (Highland) Division, preparing for a big offensive, which would be known as the Battle of Arras.

At the Front he kept a diary of short observations that paint a vivid picture of the conflict those at home were working hard to supply:

> 'Ammunition dump shelled and exploded. Working day and night, shrapnel everywhere ... The ground we walk upon shakes ... Bombardment started again, deafening roars, cannot sleep.'

He noted the heavy guns drawn by caterpillar tractors, that were probably shipped from Avonmouth. He surveyed the skies filled with aircraft, perhaps turned out from George White's factory:

> 'Aeroplane down in flames ... German aeroplanes hovering overhead all morning.'

And he gasped at the sight of shells exploding in spectacular bombardments: 'A most wonderful sight never to be forgotten' – shells that may have been touched by the fair hands of Bristol's women.

In May 1917, Hardingham climbed into a captured enemy trench:

> 'Dugouts 70ft deep. Guns etc just as it was left. Dead Germans. A man dead drunk found in a dugout ... German prisoners being brought in. One Boche about 7ft high.'

Shortly afterwards he witnessed the devastation of French civilian life.

> 'Came through Arras, what was once a beautiful town is now a mass of ruins. Pianos etc smashed up and nothing now but debris in roadway.'

Such scenes affected many troops deeply towards the end of the war.

Happily, Frederick Hardingham survived and came home to his family. He found work at a printing firm, got married again, had three more children and enjoyed showing off his party piece – tap dancing on an upturned dinner plate. But the city he returned to was now part of a world that had been changed forever.

Soldiers of the Gloucestershire Regiment survey the ruins of war.
[SoGM, Ref: GLRRM:04531.121]

Chapter Five

1918 – A Changed World

AS THE PEOPLE OF BRISTOL saw in the New Year of 1918 war had become a way of life and although some still attempted to celebrate, the optimism and stoicism that had buoyed them for so long was starting to give way to weariness and despair.

Shortages and shop queues were now routine and women cannily passed their babies around to help each other to get preferential treatment in food queues. Margarine replaced butter, bread now contained potato to save grain, and fresh meat was in short supply although frozen meat was available. Oxo placed advertisements in the local press with recipes for new types of meals, such as cabbage and chestnuts or carrots with fine herbs, and helpfully explained: 'Oxo can be used in conjunction with potatoes and other vegetables to make many inexpensive dishes which take the place of a meat course.' Many disliked having to change their ways and these were the people who complained the loudest, according to *Bristol and the Great War* which was published in 1920:

> 'There was nothing like a food famine at any time. Those who suffered most were the people who could not adapt their daily diet to the supplies that were available.'

Elsewhere, schools drafted in ageing teachers to replace younger colleagues who had gone to fight, but it was generally acknowledged that their lessons were less than inspiring. And in family homes it was feared that the demands of war were putting children's welfare at risk. Dr Madeline Baker reported to the Bristol Education Committee.

> 'Fathers are absent on military service; the mothers, either from necessity or from choice, are constantly found to be absent all the day in the factory or workshop. The elder children, and regrettably often those between 13 and 14 years of age, are also under employment and earning wages, which tend to exempt them from parental control. It is deplorably evident that the lack of discipline and cleanliness and the prevalence of diseases prolonged by dirt and neglect are increasing amongst school children.'

Infants at Air Balloon Hill School, St George. Fewer children now needed free meals.

It wasn't all bad news though. The extra work that the war generated meant more money and better living standards for the poorer classes. Fewer youngsters now had to rely on free school meals and there was a fall in the number of working class patients being treated by doctors under the National Insurance Act.

Sadly, though, cracks were beginning to emerge in marriages and relationships. 'Clara told me to tell you to go over as she wants another kiss in the passage,' wrote Florence Cottle, of Easton, to her soldier husband. 'Her own boy have [sic] done the dirty on her, she said, and

haven't wrote for over a month [*sic*].'

The courts in Bristol were having to deal with cases of unfaithful wives, bigamous husbands – and worse. In October 1917 a sensation was caused when a soldier shot his wife dead and the *Bristol Evening News* couldn't wait to divulge the details:

'Early this morning a terrible tragedy occurred at Temple Meads Railway Station, the victim being Mrs Bessie Cross, the young wife of a soldier named Albert John Cross, of the Gloucester Regiment. The sensational incident occurred shortly after 1 am.'

The report breathlessly continued:

'It appeared that Cross, who is in custody on a charge of wilful murder, had been home on ten days leave from France and was about to return to the front. It is said his wife went to see him off, and having missed the earlier train, they were waiting for one timed to go about 3 am. Suddenly a rifle shot rang out and some military police hastened to the spot where they found the unfortunate young woman dying on the platform. She had been shot right through the lower portion of the body and was taken in a dying condition to the Bristol General Hospital, where she expired soon afterwards.'

At the inquest it was revealed that Bessie Cross had been carrying the child of another man named as James King, who was married with 'eight or nine' children of his own. The jury returned a verdict of 'wilful murder under great provocation' and described King's conduct as 'most reprehensible, he being responsible for all the trouble'.

When Albert Cross went on trial crowds queued to get into the court. As he stood in the dock looking pale and dressed in khaki, yet more personal details were revealed. The court heard that King had sent a letter to Cross in the trenches explaining that he had nothing more to do with his wife, who was now 'misconducting herself' with other men. Cross had written to King accusing him of 'hunting down and ruining women whose husbands were serving their country, and poor widows, who had lost their husbands in the war.'

As this sad case drew to a close, a final witness took to the stand and said that when Cross pulled the trigger at Temple Meads Station he had shown no emotion. The court took the view that he had been pushed too far and acquitted him of wilful murder.

* * *

Whatever the ups and downs of domestic life, Bristol's newspapers remained cheerfully patriotic and were vital in keeping spirits high. However hopeless people felt, they could rely on the *Times and Mirror*, the *Evening News* and the *Western Daily Press* to reassure them that the Germans must be defeated and that the Allies would prevail. No story was too small to be reported if it told of locals doing their bit. No serviceman was too insignificant to be mentioned in reports from the Front or casualty lists.

The city even had its own magazine that was devoted to the conflict, *Bristol and the Great War* (not to be confused with the 1920 book of the same name), which was sold at home and abroad where Bristolians were stationed. Readers were encouraged to get in touch with their news, stories and photos.

Newspapers had troubles of their own, however, with paper shortages and rising costs forcing many to reduce their size. Some weekday editions of the *Bristol Times and Mirror* consisted of just two printed sides in 1918 and proprietors offered to pay readers for waste paper that could be recycled. Unfortunately some local journals had to close, like *Frenchay Church Magazine*. It was announced in 1918:

> 'Owing to the high price of paper and the great increase in the cost of printing, the expenses of a monthly issue amounted to about three times the receipts from the sale of the magazines, and it is not possible to meet so large a deficit out of the Churchwardens' Fund.'

The magazine was re-started after the war.

Newspapers brought the war into everyone's living rooms but it was still a shock when the conflict came close to home. On 26 February 1918 a hospital ship was torpedoed by a German submarine in the Bristol Channel, just off Lundy Island, with the loss of 153 lives. Reports said the *Glenart Castle* sank in just seven minutes, stern first, 'with a thunderous roar of surging waters'. Piercing shrieks were heard coming from the sea, according to one survivor.

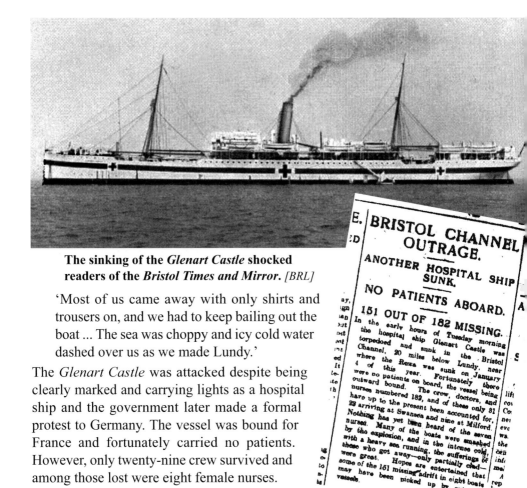

The sinking of the *Glenart Castle* shocked readers of the *Bristol Times and Mirror*. [BRL]

'Most of us came away with only shirts and trousers on, and we had to keep bailing out the boat ... The sea was choppy and icy cold water dashed over us as we made Lundy.'

The *Glenart Castle* was attacked despite being clearly marked and carrying lights as a hospital ship and the government later made a formal protest to Germany. The vessel was bound for France and fortunately carried no patients. However, only twenty-nine crew survived and among those lost were eight female nurses.

Two weeks later the same almost happened again when the *Guildford Castle*, another hospital ship and sister ship of the *Glenart Castle*, was targeted by U-Boats in the Bristol Channel. This vessel was returning to port with 500 wounded and 500 crew when it was struck by a torpedo, but fortunately no damage was caused and nobody was hurt.

* * *

Even during the darkest moments of the war, Bristolians still managed to make the best of things. Old photographs show that people weren't afraid to enjoy themselves, especially when they were entertaining wounded

A tonic for the troops, Bristolians excelled when it came to entertaining wounded soldiers. *[Jack Williams]*

soldiers, which was something the city had always done well. There were trips on the river, excursions by motorcycle and motorcar, matinee performances at cinemas and theatres, and memorable days out at Clifton Zoological Gardens

Many events for the wounded were overseen by an organisation that is hardly remembered today but did an immense amount of work in Bristol and was run like a well-oiled machine. The Inquiry Bureau began life as a small band of volunteers that was set up to answer inquiries about wounded soldiers in city hospitals (thus explaining its rather sinister-sounding name). As the war progressed, it expanded to oversee just about everything a wounded soldier could ask for: arranging lodgings for visiting relatives, advising on gratuities and pensions, re-training for life after the war, organising Christmas parties. Volunteers also interviewed wounded men to find out what had happened to those who were missing in action. The bureau kept a meticulous card-index system, carefully cross-referenced and updated, and by the end of the war there were half-a-million names recorded.

A grand day out at Clifton Zoo for recovering soldiers and their fun-loving female hosts. *[Jack Williams]*

The Inquiry Bureau may have sounded rather formal but it was far from stuffy. When word reached Bristol that London was claiming a record for clearing 2,000 wounded men from an entertainment hall in just one hour, the bureau rose to the challenge. With military precision it oversaw the speedy exit of 2,200 wounded from the Bristol Hippodrome, including 350 on crutches, in just thirty-seven minutes. So much for health and safety.

* * *

Understandably, fun and laughter wasn't what every serviceman wanted to see when he arrived home on leave. It didn't take much for some to feel their efforts at the Front weren't being appreciated. 'If you had any idea what life was like in the trenches, you would think twice before being so gay and light-hearted,' wrote one local newspaper correspondent. Another unwelcome surprise may have been to see just how well the American allies were settling in at home.

The United States had entered the war in 1917 when its merchant ships came under attack from German U-Boats. Hundreds of wounded Americans would be invalided back to the city and a café-lounge was opened specially for them at Carlton Chambers in Baldwin Street. There were also plenty of American airmen stationed north of the city at Yate, and 300 of them caught the train to Bristol on 4 July to take part in a huge Independence Day parade.

The Americans never had to look far for attention. 'The girls came miles to see us as if we were a circus and the Tommies were out of luck if one of us Yank curiosities could be found for an escort,' wrote Corporal Ned Steel of Kansas City, who was stationed at Yate. He was amazed at how bold the Bristol women were and wrote (with American translations in brackets):

> 'What quite took our breath away was to have a pretty girl bum us for an American cigarette, or in a "pub" (saloon) buy the treats of ale for us and think nothing of it. And when a "flapper" (Broadway chicken) in Bristol looked offended if we failed to kiss her goodbye (though we had just chanced to meet her ten minutes before) we nearly fell over. These habits, we were told, were the result of the war.'

Corporal Steel belonged to the American 822nd (Repair) Squadron, one of several US units sent to England to learn how to repair damaged

American airmen, seen here opening their mail at Yate, proved very popular with the ladies. *[Y&DHC]*

aircraft before moving on to France. When he arrived in April 1918, Steel was fairly scornful of the British – their cooking came in for criticism, so too did the slackness in the workshop when nobody in authority was around, and the way every second word seemed to be 'bloody'.

However, when his squadron departed for France ten weeks later Steel had new-found respect. The expertise he had observed in the aircraft workshops impressed him and so did the sacrifices that ordinary people had made for the war. Waving goodbye to the girls who came to see them off, he reflected:

> 'Nearly every one of them had lost brothers or other dear ones in the long never-ending war. Then, could you blame them for crying softly as they watched the train move away?'

* * *

At the beginning of 1918 all talk was of a big spring offensive being planned by the Germans on the Western Front. As people braced themselves for yet more slaughter, newly married Florence Cottle of Easton breathed a sigh of relief when her husband Grantley arrived back to England with a shoulder wound. 'I don't know whether I feel ten years younger or 10 stone lighter but I feel a different girl since I read your letter yesterday and knew your [*sic*] in Blighty once more,' she wrote. 'I thank God you've been spared to come back and I hope before long the war will be over and we shall be in our own little paradise.'

Florence's letters of 1918 suggest there was now little appetite for patriotism. Women just wanted their men home. 'You must swing the leg [*sic*] kidder and hang on as long as possible,' she urged Grantley in hospital. In the same letter she said her friend's husband was being treated for blood poisoning in France: 'He can't walk as his ankles give way, but she wrote and told him to keep falling down.' Florence was sometimes surprised that her letters were passed by the censors, but perhaps they too had had enough of war.

The great spring offensive was finally launched in March 1918 and for once the *Bristol Times and Mirror* was less than bullish about the Allies' prospects. 'THE NEW GERMAN BLOW' is how it broke the news to its readers. 'Attack delivered in dense

The Lord Mayor of Bristol Henry Twiggs: 'The future of the world is at stake'.
[Bristol and the Great War , Wells and Stone, 1920]

mist, fierce hand-to-hand struggle – this morning's news by telegraph and telephone.' As the Allies were forced to retreat, Bristolians were urged to pray for fifteen minutes each day, at 1pm, at churches that would be open for the purpose. 'The future of the world is at stake,' wrote the bishop and the mayor in a letter to the local press.

The offensive would drag on for many months and initially the Allies lost a lot of ground. But as morale declined among exhausted German soldiers, the Allies countered with a series of decisive victories and by August the end was in sight. 'A crushing victory certain,' trumpeted the *Bristol Times and Mirror* with restored confidence. It continued with a deck of rousing headlines:

'Great Stroke by Haig'

'Hundreds of tanks employed'

'Advance to depth of 7 miles'

'Cavalry's magnificent work'

'Fleeing Huns cut down and villages captured'

'Over 100 guns and 700 prisoners'

Douglas Haig, the former Clifton College boy who was now commander of the British Army in France, had urged his men to fight on to the end and he was credited with much of the success in the final months on the Western Front. A letter of congratulation was sent to him by Sir Herbert Warren, chairman of the council of Clifton College, and Haig replied: 'It is a source of great pride and pleasure that our fortunes out here are followed with such generous appreciation by my old school.' Haig was later awarded the freedom of the City of Bristol.

* * *

The armistice was signed on Monday, 11 November 1918 and the announcement reached the Boucher household in Tyndall's Park Road, Clifton, rather earlier than expected. Maude Boucher wrote in her wartime scrapbook:

> 'We had been thinking that we shouldn't get the news until the evening so when the old man who delivers our newspapers, came here in the morning and said that news had just come through that the Germans had signed the peace terms, we could scarcely believe it was true.'

The centre of Bristol was alive with celebration. The sound of factory hooters, ships' horns and church bells were everywhere. Bands of

GERMANY'S HUMILIATION.

EVACUATION TO THE RHINE.

ALLIES TO OCCUPY BRIDGEHEADS.

ALL U-BOATS TO SURRENDER.

WARSHIPS TO DISARM: 5,000 GUNS FOR ALLIES.

RIGHT TO OCCUPY HELIGOLAND.

REPATRIATION WITHOUT RECIPROCITY

The great world war came to an end yesterday at 11 a.m. Yesterday was the 100th day of the fifth year. The following historic announcement was issued by Mr. Lloyd George at 10.20 yesterday morning.

THE ARMISTICE WAS SIGNED AT 5 a.m. THIS MORNING, AND HOSTILITIES ARE TO CEASE ON ALL FRONTS AT 11 a.m. TO-DAY.

Immediately following the signing of the armistice the following message was sent out by wireless:—

Marshal Foch to Commanders-in-Chief.

Hostilities will cease on the whole front as from November 11th at 11 o'clock (French time).

The Allied troops will not, until a further order, go beyond the line reached on that date and at that hour.

(Signed)   MARSHAL FOCH.

The acceptance by Germany of the Allies' terms (the full text of which will be found below) means the end of the war, as the safeguards included will make it impossible for Germany to renew the struggle.

News of the armistice is triumphantly announced by the *Bristol Times and Mirror*. [BRL]

ragamuffins, some without boots, marched up Clare Street with a union flag, singing popular war songs and beating battered tin cans. Workers snatched up their hats and coats and disappeared into the throng, many did not return for the rest of the week. Wine merchants were under siege by people eager to buy champagne. Groups of cheering men hailed taxi-cabs and urged them to drive up and down Park Street as fast as possible.

Owners later took their cabs off the streets for fear they would break down.

For Maude Boucher, who had lost a brother at the Front, it was a time for reflection:

'It is difficult to describe what one's feelings were at such a time – but you felt that you wanted to go out and join in all the excitement and enthusiasm with other people ... There was the great feeling of relief that the fighting – with the terrible loss of life – was now over.'

Newspaper reporters who, back in 1914, could hardly contain their excitement at the outbreak of war were now more circumspect:

'Quite early in the day labour was suspended at most of our leading industrial establishments – thus relieving the Lord Mayor from the responsibility of proclaiming a holiday – and the employees trooped out to join in impromptu demonstrations and to take their share in the rejoicings which continued till the night was reached ... Restraint underlay the enthusiasm without spoiling its wholeheartedness.'

The Lord Mayor Henry Twiggs also adopted a sombre tone when he addressed waiting crowds outside the Council House: 'We are devoutly thankful that the last shot has been fired and we can look forward to welcoming back our boys to their homes.'

* * *

Prime Minister David Lloyd George had promised servicemen that they would return to a land fit for heroes to live in, but in reality nothing could have been further from the truth. Civilians had been through a gruelling four years too and were struggling to come to terms with what had happened. There was little inclination to put one section of society on a pedestal. 'Thus come we out of the furnace of affliction to face a yet greater trial, that of success,' were the prophetic words of the *Frenchay Church Magazine* when it resumed publication in January 1919.

The great homecoming brought with it a devastating influenza epidemic during the winter of 1918-19, which killed millions worldwide. Known as Spanish flu, the virus had found an ideal breeding ground in the fetid trenches and was spread by returning soldiers. Warning bells sounded in Bristol that November when theatres, music halls and cinemas

FLU

has been conspicuous by its absence in homes where

FIRST AID

is regularly used.

FIRST AID is the scientific disinfectant soap of guaranteed power. It is made in a unique way, and its value in combating microbe-borne disease can hardly be over-estimated.

In triple tablets, 7½d.

Made only by Christr. Thomas & Bros. Ltd., Bristol

★The First Aid Book, 40 pp. of illustrated first aid hints, free on request if usual dealer's name mentioned.

Some advertisers saw the flu epidemic as an opportunity to grab customers.
[BRL Bristol Times and Mirror]

were declared out of bounds to the military. Few escaped the virus, even the lady mayoress was too ill to attend one official engagement with her husband. Thankfully most people recovered, but by January 1919 the number of deaths in Bristol had reached 1,050. At the Beaufort War Hospital, thirty out of 164 deaths recorded there during the entire war were due to influenza.

Servicemen came home in dribs and drabs with many remaining in Europe until the following year to 'mop up', but some would never be the same again. One young girl recalled watching the soldiers from a local hospital sunning themselves at Leigh Woods:

'One was always brought there on a stretcher by the orderlies. He was fair-haired, young and handsome, and always laughing. I was about 11 at the time and I asked my mother why he was all wrapped up like that. She told me he had lost both arms and both legs.'

The first to be demobilised were often those with jobs to come back to and Arthur Kendall was one of many who had reason to be grateful to their pre-war employers for providing letters like this: 'The Metal Agencies Company Limited of Queen Square, Bristol, hereby declare that Private A.C. Kendall 265826 High Street, Staple Hill, Bristol was in our employment before August 4th 1914 and that we are prepared to offer him employment as a clerk immediately on his return to civilian life.'

But unemployment was a big problem in Bristol, as it was all over the country, because businesses that had once been busy supplying the war now had to lay off staff. There was also the added problem that women

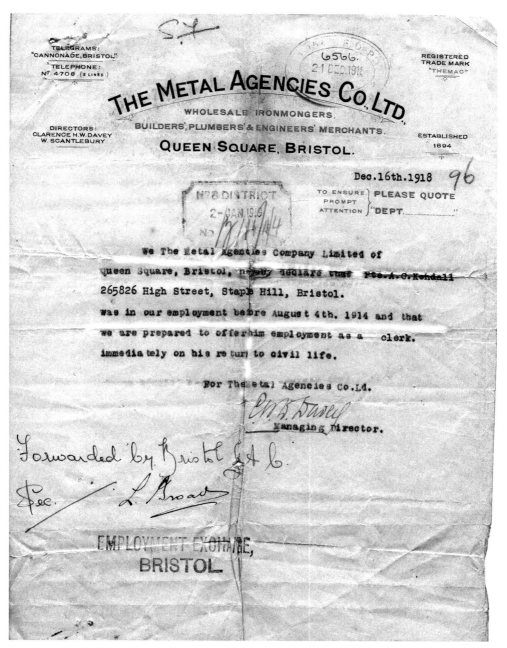

A promise of post-war employment for Bristol soldier Arthur Kendall.
[SoGM, Ref: GLRRM: 04531.1]

Castle Green Girls' Club provided good training for young ladies in pre-war Bristol ... *[BRL, Ref F551ii Samuel Loxton]*

filled many jobs that once belonged to men – and not all returning soldiers were prepared to stand aside now that war was over.

As more and more were demobilised, so stories of destitute ex-servicemen became common and discontent spread. It simmered threateningly for months and finally erupted in April 1920 with ugly protests in the city centre against the women conductors on Bristol's trams. The clippies had been taken on by Bristol Tramways and Carriage Company to replace some of the 2,280 men who went to war. By mid 1919 only 650 ex-servicemen had been re-employed. During near riots, trams were vandalised and women conductors were abused and jeered at. With further action threatened Bristol Tramways succumbed and dismissed its remaining female employees, paying them £5 to go without a fuss.

Despite the humbling of the clippies, the freedom and responsibility that women had enjoyed during the war planted seeds of liberation just as

... but now they were having too much fun to bother with cookery classes.
[Jack Williams]

surely as the suffragette movement had. No longer did they feel obliged to be submissive and properly behaved. On Armistice Day, for example, one surprised onlooker was shocked to see 'girls dressed in soldiers' uniforms and smoking round the town, also land girls rolling drunk'!

Some women would still choose to put duty before liberation and offered themselves as wives to soldiers who were disfigured or badly wounded. Early on in the war one former Weston-super-Mare schoolgirl had volunteered for a painful skin graft so that an officer could return to the Front. Nellie Vincent – 'a charming young lady scarcely out of her teens', according to the local paper – answered this newspaper advertisement: 'Officer requires 4in by 3in of skin to cover wound and expedite his return to duty; opportunity for unselfish patriot.' Nellie is reported to have said:

> 'I am quite willing to give what is needed and should be only too pleased to do so. The soldier did a good deal for us and I think there should be scores of offers in a case like this.'

But as servicemen began returning home, it became apparent that it was not only bodies that were in need of repair. Many men's minds had been horribly damaged too.

Francis Clutterbuck grew up in Berkeley on the banks of the Severn Estuary north of Bristol, where his parents ran a village pub and his father worked on the local estates. As a boy Francis learned to play the organ and was good enough to try out the one at Gloucester Cathedral. When he left school he worked as an apprentice to a mechanical engineer in Lydney, in the Forest of Dean, but thereafter life became less predictable.

When war broke out Francis ran away to join the army with his younger brother George and another friend from Berkeley. All were underage. In 1914 Francis was aged 16 and George was a year younger. Little is known about their war experiences but when Francis eventually returned he was in deep shock, traumatised and unable to move. Classified as an incurable paralytic, brain surgery was recommended at the hospital where he was being treated, but his mother consulted with her Berkeley GP who urged her to say no. He was convinced that doctors wanted to use soldiers like Clutterbuck as guinea pigs for their research. Instead he suggested another technique that he had heard about, hypnosis.

Under treatment Clutterbuck broke down and revealed what had previously been locked inside him. That during one tremendous battle he had seen his friend from Berkeley sliced in half by an exploding shell.

Clutterbuck was badly wounded and lay helpless among the dead until an officer on horseback saw him throw his arm backwards and managed to get him to an aid station. Once he could speak about what had happened, Clutterbuck was encouraged to start playing the piano again, which helped him regain movement. After the war he was able to resume a normal life but would always need to have residual shrapnel removed from his head and body as it worked its way to the surface.

Not all were as fortunate. Ernest Brake came from a large family in the St Jude's area of Bristol and at the age of 19 enlisted with his brother Dennis. He served on the Western Front as a gunner with an artillery

Ernest Brake as a servicemen, and in later life at Glenside Hospital. *[The Brake Family]*

battery equipped with howitzers that lobbed heavy shells at high angles into the German trenches. Whether the deafening noise, the constant dangers of enemy counter-bombardment, or the gas attacks he suffered became too much, nobody knows. But when Brake was discharged from the army in May 1919 he was suffering from shell shock.

Initially he was sent to the Dorset County Asylum at Dorchester, then moved to Glenside Hospital at Fishponds (formerly the Beaufort War Hospital) where he spent the rest of his life.

'It was as if he blocked out the war and went back to his childhood,' said his niece Betty Siddell. 'It could well have been a type of amnesia as he never had anything to say to anyone but would respond to his siblings if told to do something.' His life wasn't unhappy at the hospital – with twelve brothers and sisters (although not Dennis, who was killed in August 1918) he was never short of family members to take him out at the weekend. He died in 1979.

Soldiers displaying the symptoms of shell shock were often accused of lacking moral fibre and some were even shot for cowardice. However, important steps were being made to prove that sufferers were not malingerers and that war neuroses, as it was known, really did exist. One of the pioneers in this field was a man who later became a well-respected resident of Frenchay, Professor Frederick Golla. The grandson of an Italian count, he was an eminent neuro-psychiatrist who served as an officer in the Royal Army Medical Corps during the war. What he saw in the trenches greatly influenced his views. While some experts considered shell shock to be psychological trauma, Golla believed it was the result of physiological damage to the nervous system and that some people were more prone than others. In his experience, there was 'little difficulty in spotting the future cases of neurosis before even a shot was fired'. Tantalizingly, he didn't say exactly how such cases could be identified.

Golla served on many committees that looked into the effects of trench warfare. He moved to Frenchay in 1939 when he was appointed the first director of the renowned Burden Neurological Institute, based at the former Stoke Park Hospital. He remained in the village for the rest of his life until he died in 1968, aged 89.

* * *

It would be a mistake to think all homecomings were fraught with difficulty. Some servicemen were able to relish the simple pleasures in

**Professor
Frederick Golla,
who carried out
pioneering work
into shell shock.**
[FVM]

Womens Royal Air Force, No3 (W.
Yate, July 191

The Women's Royal Air Force at Yate in a formal line-up, July 1918.
[Y&DHC]

life again despite their experiences. Edwin Bigwood, whose family came from Clifton and ran a building business, witnessed more than his fair share of horror at the Front but had the happy knack of brushing trauma aside once it was over. Recalling an incident in 1917 when he and a small

R.D. R.A.F.

group of soldiers were stranded on high ground at the mercy of the enemy, he later recalled an amusing tale:

'We ran very short of ammunition and were grubbing around for spare rounds when someone shouted out, "Have you found some, Bigwood?" Then a very tall young soldier said, "How strange, your name is Bigwood, my name's Littlewood!" He was over 6ft tall, and I was 5ft 4?.'

TAKEN AT
POPERHINGE
Oct 1917

Bigwood was invalided back to England in January 1918 after being struck in the face by shrapnel and was sent to Wharncliffe War Hospital, Sheffield.

'I spent six happy months here, especially on a Sunday afternoon when I used to go with a Cockney to a pub called the Cross Hands at Handsworth, where we had tea. Mrs Goddard (a widow) had four charming daughters, but amazingly we were not interested – it was just the homeliness and perhaps the pianolas which we enjoyed playing, after the pub was closed.'

* * *

In their letters home, soldiers often expressed pity for the people of France and Belgium whose lives and countries had been torn apart. There was quiet gratitude that Britain had not suffered in the same way. But the war

Edwin Bigwood, left, relished simple pleasures when he returned home, but there was pity for the people of France, above, whose lives had been torn apart. *[Bigwood Family / David Clark]*

had still wrought huge and unexpected changes, and one of the most profound was the crumbling of the class system. The old structures of society were still firmly in place in 1914, recalled Louise Powell, a lifelong resident of Frenchay who was 8 when war broke out:

> 'In those days Frenchay was composed of large Georgian houses housing the gentry, cottages where the working class lived and a few others who fitted into neither category.'

Looking back decades later she said the conflict was a prelude to the transition that lifted Frenchay out of its feudal way of life and into the modern world.

A more subtle change in old traditions was observed by a sporting onlooker at Clifton College: 'It may be worth while to call to attention an innovation which has crept in this term, I mean the practice of shouting at football [rugby football] matches,' he wrote in the *Cliftonian* magazine in December 1918.

'The habit of abstaining from any form of applause except

The entrance to Yate prisoner-of-war camp, where up to 1,000 inmates were held. *[Y&DHC]*

clapping has long been a source of wonder, not to say admiration,
to outsiders who have come to regard this Clifton characteristic
as evidence of an amount of self-restraint quite unusual among a
body of schoolboys.'

Perhaps spectators had now adopted the noisier habits of Association
Football, which had become so popular during the war.

The countryside surrounding Bristol also bore the marks of a changed
world, nowhere more so than at Yate where wartime development helped
to reshape the old farming landscape. A huge aerodrome had been
constructed on farmland north of Station Road, which provided a base for
the Royal Flying Corps (later the Royal Air force) that could
accommodate 2,000 personnel, including women of the new Women's
Royal Air Force.

The aerodrome was built using labour from a German prisoner-of-war
camp that stood to the east of Westerleigh Road, between what is now
Stanshawes Drive and Brookthorpe. As many as 1,000 prisoners could be
held there. The camp was one of several dotted around the countryside,
which provided workers where they were needed locally. Forty prisoners

were held at Marlwood Grange, Thornbury. Another fifty worked at nearby Tytherington stone quarries, although these were civilians – mainly Austrians – who were interned at the outbreak of war because they were deemed a risk to national security.

German prisoners were generally accepted by the locals although there was some antagonism. It was reported that labourers at Hawkesbury Upton had threatened to down tools if Germans came on to their farms to work. The people of Thornbury were happier to accept foreign help although their tolerance wasn't always reciprocated. In July 1918 a German named George Hennecke, 21, escaped from Thornbury camp and went on the run. He was last seen wearing a brown tunic, blue trousers with red stripe and dark grey overcoat, reported the *Western Times*.

At Penpole camp near Shirehampton, it seems that some prisoners got on very well with the locals. Otto Muller befriended one girl and gave her a signed card, dated 20 September 1919, which was later discovered in a local archive. Another German prisoner touched the heart of a mother when he was working at a park in Kings Weston. 'I have a little girl like her at home,' said the prisoner, before asking if he could touch her child. 'My mother said he could, forgetting for that moment the fact that he was the enemy,' the young girl later recalled.

Local girls, like these at Eastville Park, touched the hearts of German prisoners who had daughters of their own at home.

All change: when the children of Frenchay watched their fathers depart for war, the village was full of Edwardian certainty. Four years later the social hierarchy had started to crumble and women like these in the WRAF canteen at Yate were now at ease in a man's world. *[Y&DHC]*

EPILOGUE

IT WASN'T UNTIL SPRING FINALLY ARRIVED in 1919 that people's thoughts turned to commemorating those who had died. Sixty thousand Bristol men had enlisted during the war and 4,400 never returned. Most were buried where they fell (if they were ever found) for there were simply too many bodies to bring home.

It would take years for Bristol to reach agreement about the city's civic war memorial. Disputes over funding and location created delays that meant the Cenotaph in Colston Avenue wasn't unveiled until 1932. Meanwhile, parishes and villages drew up plans for their own memorials, meetings were held to decide what form they should take, sketches were submitted to planners and stonemasons set to work. Dates were arranged for them to be dedicated and unveiled and the local newspapers reported it all with care. A memorial cross for St John's Church, Clifton (November 1919); proposals to restore a churchyard cross at Yatton, south of Bristol (December 1919); the dedication of Stoke Bishop war memorial cross on the Downs, at the top of Stoke Hill (May 1920).

One hundred years later Bristol's war memorials, once bright and newly carved, have settled back into the landscape like ancient roadside crosses, silently guarded by lists of sleeping men.

Resting place of some of the brave Bristol Territorials who have fallen.

Buried where they fell: Bristol territorial soldiers at peace in a graveyard in France *[BRL, Bristol and the War magazine]*

Bibliography

Beeson A., *Bristol Central Library and Charles Holden, a History and Guide*, Redcliffe Press, Bristol, 2006

Birdwood Field Marshal Lord, *Khaki and Gown – an Autobiography*, Ward Lock, 1941

Bristol Cultural Development Partnership, *The 2010 Book of Aviation Wonder*, BCDP, 2010

Bulmer R.H. (ed), *Frenchay – A Village at War*, Frenchay Tuckett Society, Frenchay, 2012 (second edition)

Bulmer R.H., *H.J. Wadlow of Frenchay National School*, Frenchay Tuckett Society, Frenchay, 2003

Burlton C., *Trenches to Trams – The Life of a Bristol Tommy*, Tangent Books, Bristol, 2011

Crowther S., Dickson A., Truscoe K., *Severn Estuary Rapid Coastal Zone Assessment Survey: National Mapping Programme*, Gloucestershire County Council, English Heritage, Somerset County Council, 2008

Christie O.F., *A History of Clifton College, 1860-1934*, J.W. Arrowsmith, Bristol, 1935

Cooper Dr R., *Professor Golla of Frenchay and the Burden Institute*, Frenchay Tuckett Society, Frenchay, 2002

Doyle P., *The British Soldier of the First World War*, Shire Publications Ltd, Oxford, 2008

Doyle P., *First World War Britain*, Shire Publications Ltd, Oxford, 2012

Eveleigh D.J., *Britain in Old Photographs – Bristol 1850-1919*, Sutton Publishing Ltd, Stroud, 1996

Gough P. (ed), *Your Loving Friend, Stanley: The Great War Correspondence Between Stanley Spencer and Desmond Chute*, Sansom & Co, 2011

Haig The Countess, *The Man I Knew, The Intimate Life-Story of Douglas Haig*, Moray Press, 1935

Lyes J. *Bristol 1914-1919*, Bristol Branch of the Historical Association, 2003

Marks D., *'Bristol's Own' – The 12th Battalion Gloucestershire Regiment 1914-1918*, Dolman Scott Ltd, Bristol, 2011

Neale W.G., *The Tides of War and the Port of Bristol 1914-1918*, Port

Of Bristol Authority, 1976

Penny J., *Bristol at Work*, Breedon Books Publishing Co Ltd, Derby, 2005

Thomas E., *War Story*, E.Thomas, Bristol, 1989

Thornicroft N., *Gloucestershire and North Bristol – Soldiers on the Somme,* Tempus Publishing Ltd Stroud, 2007

Scott D. (ed), *Douglas Haig: The Preparatory Prologue Diaries and Letters 1861-1914*, Pen and Sword Military, Barnsley, 2006

Storey N.R. and Housego M., *Women in the first World War*, Shire Publications Ltd, Oxford, 2013

Stephenson D., *The History of Lawrence Hill* (booklet)

Wells C. and G.F. Stone (eds), *Bristol and the Great War*, J.W. Arrowsmith Ltd, Bristol, 1920

Williams J. and Humphries C., *Mother Keeps a Mangle, Memories of East Bristol*, privately published, Bristol, 2008

Woods D., *Bristol City – The Early Years*, Desert Island Books Ltd, Southend-on-Sea, 2004

Woods D., *Bristol City – From War to War 1915-1946*, Desert Island Books Ltd, Southend-on-Sea, 2008

Other Research Sources

I received valuable help from the organisations listed below. Websites are included where appropriate. Initials show the abbreviations I have used on picture credits.

Airbus, Bristol

The Bristol Port Company, Avonmouth

Bristol Record Office http://archives.bristol.gov.uk/dserve/
The BRO holds the Maude Boucher Scrapbooks (Ref No 44859) and the Florence Cottle Letters (Ref No 44775), both of which have been used in this book

Bristol Reference Library (BRL)
http://www.bristol.gov.uk/page/leisure-and-culture/central-library-reference-services

Clifton College, Bristol

Frenchay Village Museum (FVM)
http://www.frenchaymuseumarchives.co.uk/

Glenside Hospital Museum, Stapleton, Bristol **(GHM)**

www.glensidemuseum.org.uk

Kingswood Museum http://www.kingswoodmuseum.org.uk/

The Malago Society http://www.malago.org.uk/

Myers-Insole Local Learning Community Interest Company,
Bristol http://www.locallearning.org.uk/allourstories.html

Sandham Memorial Chapel, Berkshire
http://www.nationaltrust.org.uk/sandham-memorial-chapel/

Shirehampton Book of Remembrance website
http://shirehamptonbookofremembrance.webs.com/

Soldiers of Gloucestershire Museum, Custom House, Gloucester
Docks **(SOGM)** http://www.glosters.org.uk/

Thornbury Museum http://www.thornburymuseum.org.uk/

Yate and District Heritage Centre (Y&DHC)
http://www.yateheritage.co.uk/

American Airman Ned Steel's quotes are taken from *History of the
Squadron – originally the 822nd (Repair), later the 6th Park Co, at
present the 6th Air Park,* a copy of which is held by the Y&DHC

Index